A Roller Coaster, A Roundabout, and A Road Trip

Three Exciting Rides That Will Change Your Life

Elizabeth Murphy

To Kelly —
Many blessings,
Elizabeth

xulon PRESS

To Michael, it was my turn the moment I met you.

A Roller Coaster, A Roundabout, and A Road Trip

Three Exciting Rides That Will Change Your Life

Introduction

How to Use This Book

W hy a book on the Magi *for women*? To start with, the visit of the Magi is an ancient story familiar to women of almost every faith tradition. That's one of the things that drew me to the topic for this book – every woman has heard the story at one time or another – and you probably even have the Magi sitting in your living room every Christmas! I originally intended to write a small gift book that went along with a Christmas message I wrote a few years ago called *Follow the Star*. It was about following the star, but as I began to write it and study it, it became so much more. In fact, I was a bit shocked to find that I had so much in common with a man like Herod or that I struggled with the same things as the chief priests and teachers of the law. As I studied these men, I found myself in each of them and it not only surprised me, but challenged me. They have much to teach us as modern women living in modern times.

It's my prayer that as you read this book it will challenge you, too. As you travel through the pages, look for yourself in the characters, asking God what He might want to teach you, how He might want you to look at the Bible differently seeing its relevance to your daily life. The struggles of the characters in Matthew, chapter 2 are the same struggles we, as women, face every day as we find ourselves like Herod, screaming on a roller coaster, like the chief priests and teachers of the law, dizzy in a roundabout and like the Magi, lost on a road trip.

The first five chapters tell the story and provide in-depth study. They will help you get to know the characters better, seeing yourself differently, and then have a chance to keep traveling as you work through the questions at the end of each chapter either on your own or with a group.

Chapter six identifies lessons learned along the way. It has terms that will be helpful as landmarks and suggestions for getting you back on track when you get lost. Hang on — you're in for the ride of your life!

Thanks for choosing to travel with me,

Elizabeth

Chapter 1

Moon on the Move – The Journey Begins

Road Trip

There are many different ways to take a road trip. The ones I grew up with were highly organized excursions in the family car. We had assigned seats, for the first few miles anyway, until the fighting began or someone threatened to throw up if they weren't moved to the front. We traveled with a well-stocked cooler and a trip specific map always beginning with the end in mind. Unlike the trips families take these days, we looked at the scenery, listened to my dad's choice of radio stations, and played the alphabet game.

The road trips I took in college were more free-spirited adventures. We gathered a random group of friends, piled into a barely functioning vehicle, and set off. No destination necessary. We had a full tank of gas, spare change for expenses, and time on our hands. I remember both fondly. The road trip I took in writing this book fits somewhere between those two extremes. I began with the end in mind, discovering a fresh understanding of a life of worship — the kind of life I'm designed to live — but I didn't set out to make something happen, instead something happened to me.

It began with a pickup truck ride to middle school one morning in the fall. One of my sons was doing a study of the moon for seventh-grade science. This project involved looking at the moon every day for a few weeks and keeping a daily observation log. He had to fill in boxes on a chart with drawings of the daily changes the moon goes through on the way from quarter to half to ultimately full moon and the stages in between. I was driving him to school when he asked me, with a bit of panic in his voice, to pull over. We've had lots of reasons to pull over during the raising of four boys, not many of them pleasant, so I responded quickly. It alarmed me a little as I sat, in my pajamas and my husband's big shoes, watching him lower the window, hopping up on the edge of the frame and leaning out dangerously far. When I asked what he was doing he replied, "Homework." I recognized this homework, my older sons had done the exact same project but they had kept their moon charts on the dining room table by a large window and filled it out before they went to bed at night. This son was different; he kept his chart on the floor of the truck, looked at it first thing in the morning, and checked out the moon on the move.

When I asked if he could always see it he said, "No, there are times when the weather is bad and you can't see it because of clouds. Then there are those times every once in a while when the earth gets in the way and blocks the view." "The earth gets in the way?" I repeated." "Yeah, you know it gets between me and the moon and keeps me from seeing what I need to see," he replied, as if this was totally obvious. I was silent the rest of the way to school realizing it *was* totally obvious. In his casual middle school way, my son had just hit on a deep spiritual truth. The earth in his mind equaled the world in mine, often getting between me and God, and keeping me from seeing what I need, and want, to see. My priorities get out of order and I begin to worship all the wrong things. The more I lean into the culture around me, the farther I lean away from my heavenly Father. I know from experience this is not good. It doesn't seem to matter how committed I am or even how mature in my faith I am, the pull of this world never seems to lessen.

Tripped Up

It starts with small things like over-scheduling my time. I say yes to invitations that legitimately needed a no. I am careless with my calendar and only look at the date in question rather than taking a larger look and seeing what the surrounding days and weeks involve. This leads to big things like exhaustion and depletion when everything I do, even the most fun and otherwise fulfilling things, feel like a chore. This affects my family when the overflow of my overflowing life is marked by a lack of patience and a quick temper. I look around for things that will soothe me and start with the television or a book. The next stop is usually the refrigerator followed quickly by a trip to TJ MAXX.

None of it helps. I need to see Jesus. I want to see Jesus, but when I am over controlling from trying to make things go my way, over exhausted from trying to work things out my way, and overdrawn from trying to buy the things I think will give me what I'm looking for, I become overwhelmed. Instead of looking up, at the things above, I find myself looking down, at only what is right in front of me and what affects me and mine. I can't see what I need to see because I've let the world get in the way. It's a detour I take way too often.

My son had said, "once-in-a-while," when he described how this happens with the moon. If only it were a once-in-a-while occurrence in my life. As I drove home from school that late fall day I realized a, "once-in-a-while" was coming as I saw early signs of Christmas. Christmas! We hadn't had the fall holidays yet and already we were moving into Christmas! In Wisconsin, where I live, the snow comes early and often. Some years a few enterprising people try to get outdoor decorations up before winter truly sets in. It makes sense, but could they wait until after Thanksgiving to turn on the lights?

I love Christmas, almost everything about it. The decorations, the food, the special music, the shopping, the gatherings, and the greetings — all of it. The part I love most is that at Christmas celebrations of Christ are everywhere. People that don't attend church regularly go at Christmas. Malls and all kinds of places that don't typically pay attention to the words but love the tradition of Christmas music, blast lyrics proclaiming Christ as King. There are nativity scenes in yards next to Santa Claus and Rudolph, of course, but they are there.

As a public speaker, Christmas is a busy time for me both professionally and personally. There are lots of special events where I am invited to speak, so I start early looking for funny stories and interesting facts about Christmas that I can combine with Biblical truths to make the Scriptures come alive for the women in my audiences. On my drive home from my son's school, I pondered the upcoming engagements on my calendar and decided this year was going to be different. I would begin with the Bible instead of ending up there after I had looked everywhere else for the material I would use. I wouldn't lead with culture, but would ask God if He could possibly have the most insightful thoughts, the most interesting things to say, the cleverest ideas, the most practical applications, and then trust Him to show me the way. I would give Him a chance to take me on a path I had not traveled before. One that might not send me on the shortest distance or the fastest roads or one that might involve distracting side trips and frustrating construction delays. But if I followed well and trusted the directions He gave, I would arrive at the place of peace I had been looking for and I'd have a map for my future road trips.

This kind of thinking, this new attitude could change my Christmas. It could change my life! I began by reading the book of Matthew, a logical place to start the Christmas story. When I arrived at Chapter 2, the story of the Magi, I read it over and over and began to see it differently. I knew the facts and was familiar with the events, but as I settled into the story and read slowly and carefully, pictures began forming in my mind and I saw things I had in common with the characters that I had never seen before. As I began to peek around the edges of the words on the page I realized something, this chapter in the Bible has my name written all over it. I am not like any one character all the time, but I am like all of them sometimes. I read it with fresh eyes and realized this is about so much more than Christmas — it's the story of a road trip, leading to real worship. It's a story about people who, much like me, lean too far into the culture around them, letting the world get in the way of what they need to see. This is the story of three sets of characters and their journey to Jesus.

Trip Home

Joseph and Mary, heavy with child, set out on their road trip to Bethlehem to register for the census and gave birth along the way. I guess you could say they journeyed with Jesus instead of just towards Him.

At the same time the Magi saw the babe's birth announcement star and began a road trip with destination unknown, to worship this special child.

The chief priests and teachers of the law began a road trip when they were summoned to the palace by a troubled King Herod and instructed to produce their map, the Scriptures of old, that revealed to Herod where the child would be found.

Then lastly Herod began a road trip when he lied about his intentions to worship this newborn king, and instead planned to kill him.

As I studied this chapter I realized that each of the characters in the story felt compelled for some reason to set out on this journey. The Magi were compelled by obedience, the priests and teachers first by fear of Herod and then by curiosity, and Herod by the desire for power and control. *Only* the Magi arrived at the destination, Jesus.

Herod never arrived, because he was looking for all the wrong reasons. He didn't want to know Jesus because that would reveal who he was, a false King whose rule was mostly in his mind. His life was like a roller-coaster ride he could not escape. It was filled with exhilarating ups where he felt totally in control and frightening downs that brought him face-to-face with his own powerlessness.

The priests and teachers of the law didn't find Jesus because they knew just enough about Him that they thought they knew it all. They found themselves stuck in a roundabout going in circles trying to earn the right to exit.

The Magi, however, were different. They didn't have all the knowledge they wanted, but they had what they needed — the star, and enough faith to set out in obedience. They found Jesus because they responded to His seeking star and persevered until the road ended at His feet.

Whether we realize it or not, we are all on a journey toward Jesus. Travel with me through the pages that follow and maybe you will see yourself as I did, in the heart of Herod going up and down on a roller coaster or in the performance of the priests and teachers of the law going in circles on a roundabout. It is my prayer that you won't stop there but will keep traveling as the Magi did on a road trip that ends with finding Jesus.

The Story

"After Jesus was born in Bethlehem in Judea, during the time of King Herod, Magi from the east came to Jerusalem and asked, 'Where is the one who has been

born king of the Jews? We saw his star in the east and
have come to worship him?'
When King Herod heard this he was disturbed, and
all Jerusalem with him. When he had called together
all the people's chief priests and teachers of the law,
he asked them where the Christ was to be born. 'In
Bethlehem in Judea,' they replied, 'for this is what the
prophet has written:

'But you, Bethlehem in the land of Judah,
are by no means the least among the rulers of Judah;
for out of you will come a ruler
who will be the shepherd of my people Israel.'

Then Herod called the Magi secretly and found out
from them the exact time the star had appeared. He
sent them to Bethlehem and said, 'Go and make a
careful search for the child. As soon as you find him,
report to me, so that I too may go and worship him.'
After they had heard the king, they went on their way,
and the star they had seen in the east went ahead of
them until it stopped over the place where the child
was. When they saw the star they were overjoyed.

On coming to the house, they saw the child with his mother Mary, and they bowed down and worshiped him. Then they opened their treasures and presented him with gifts of gold and of incense and of myrrh. And having been warned in a dream not to go back to Herod, they returned to their country
by another route."
Matthew 2:1-12

Keep Traveling
Chapter 1 – Moon on the Move

1. What is your favorite road trip memory?

2. How did you feel when you started?

3. What do you remember about the Magi from having heard the story in the past?

4. Who are you most interested in getting to know?
   Herod – the roller coaster rider
   The Chief Priests and Teachers of the law – the roundabout roadsters
   The Magi – the road trip travelers

Chapter 2

Discovering a Star While Gazing at the Moon
The Star

There are times in life when something someone says just sticks with you. I don't remember who the man was or the context of the show on television but I do remember the words he said, "If you look at things differently you'll see something different." It's true, so much of what we see is not about what we are looking at but *how* we are looking at it.

It's a beautiful summer day in Wisconsin as I write this. Looking out the window at the billowing white clouds, I can't help but remember all the hours I spent lying in the grass looking for cloud animals with my children. No matter what I saw, they never saw it. The boy who loved sharks always saw a shark and the boy who loved monkeys always found a monkey – sometimes one with fins! We looked at the exact same clouds in the exact same sky but because we looked at things differently, we each saw something different. Sadly no one wants to play this game with me anymore. Teenagers have better things to look at!

Star Struck

The Magi too saw a star in the sky. It could have been a comet, or planets coming together, or a legitimate star, we simply don't and won't know. What we do know; however, is that these men were astronomers, trained scientists, who studied the stars and planets. They were probably from the same priestly tribe as the prophet Daniel and had been told for generations to watch for the birth of the coming Messiah. I don't think they knew what to look for, just to keep looking. And they did — for years. As part of their daily duties they would observe the sky early in the morning and again late at night monitoring the changes, a bit like my sons and their moon charts. It was in doing this daily task of gazing at the moon that they discovered the star. An extraordinary appearance on an ordinary day. I love that God worked that way then and continues now.

The Magi weren't the only ones watching the sky, others were watching too, but the priests and religious people missed the news or misinterpreted it. The religious leaders of the day witnessed the same star-like happening, but they thought it confirmed the sovereignty of the Roman Empire and its ruler Caesar Augustus who was the greatest ruler in existence at the time. He had personal wise men in his employ and they were not interested in a promised king when they had a flesh and blood one of their own. There were celebrations all over Rome that pointed toward the greatness of Caesar which distracted these untrained observers. You could call them star struck. The world had gotten in their way and they were bowing before the wrong king. This is one of my greatest fears.

Star Sightings

I believe God still sends stars. They show up in the most unexpected and ordinary places pointing us to

Jesus. It would be easy to see them as good people, fortunate coincidences, or even dumb luck, but they aren't. They are godly people inspired by a higher calling, loving others because that's what Jesus would do. Circumstances, both good and bad, allowed by a God who wants our attention and well-placed words or tender anthems that speak the words of our hearts. They could easily be missed or misinterpreted in their simplicity, but if we pay attention, and follow well, we'll see they are stops on our road trip, our journey toward Jesus.

As I look back on my thirty-five years of following Jesus, the first star I saw in my own personal night sky was a young camp counselor in Oklahoma during the summer when I was 14. She didn't preach Jesus, she *lived* Him. She loved a bunch of blossoming teenage girls unconditionally and made us feel like peace in the midst of seemingly overwhelming problems was possible. Teenage girls can be difficult, emotional, mean spirited, and selfish – especially when they are homesick, boy crazy, and *sisters*! This counselor had me and two of my sisters in her cabin. It must have been hard to look past our teen angst and see us as beautiful, worthy, and loveable, but she did. She listened to us never once making a problem seem insignificant. She's the first person I can remember who consistently pointed me to Jesus. She obviously knew Him speaking about Him like He was her friend. She read her Bible, a lot. I had never seen anyone do that before. I was tall, awkward, and old beyond my years; she was petite, blond, and the life of the party – what a role model for me, a young woman trying to find her identity. I remember asking for her advice and rather than giving it from her own experience first, she took me to the Bible. She taught me that Jesus, in His Word, had something to say about everything. I never knew He could be so personal. The summer I spent in her cabin changed my life. I thought I wanted to be like her, but she wouldn't let me. She encouraged me to be like Jesus. She also encouraged me to systematically read through the Bible, cover to cover, praying about everything. It wasn't just what she told me to do, it was what she did. She taught me that God is knowable and wants to be known. Up until then, I had always seen God as big and distant and even a bit scary, but it was never that way for her. This precious camp friend didn't command me or even challenge me, just invited me to join her. It's a lesson I've never forgotten. We stayed in touch for years writing letters. I still have them in a box somewhere. I have no idea where she is now or what her life became, but in my mind she still sparkles for Christ.

Years later, as a married woman, I found myself looking for my identity all over again. My husband and I were relocated by his company from our home in Houston, Texas to Raleigh, North Carolina. I had given up my busy career in marketing for this move. I wasn't at all sure what I would do next, but star after star of circumstances confirmed that this was where we should go so we traveled on. We attended a church in downtown Raleigh a few weeks after we arrived and found ourselves embraced in a way that soothed our lonely souls. The first person who reached out to me was a petite dark-haired girl at church. I will call her my Southern sister. The day I met her she was surrounded by two little girls in matching dresses with giant bows in their hair. I loved them immediately. She introduced me to her husband, who looked a lot like an older brother to my husband. We became instant friends. The two things I remember about the first time we had dinner at their home were that there was not a single awkward moment in the conversation and our husbands got along as well as we did. Rare! God had put another star in my life.

My husband traveled most weeks so I was alone a lot. My new friend came to my rescue. She invited me to come over for coffee one morning and before I knew it hours had passed. We had lunch, picked up her girls from school, and eventually her husband came home for dinner. Without saying a word, she set an extra place for me. It sounds strange that I would spend hours and hours at their house, but it never felt that way to me. They literally included me in the fabric of their lives. She took me along wherever she went whether it was delivering meals on wheels or checking out a new shopping center. Our time together was equal parts serving and shopping and we laughed the whole time. We had so much in common. I have a lot in common with a lot of people, and none of them ever loved me like she did.

I watched her mother her children and love her husband with a very special devotion. She was the kind of wife and mother I wanted to be.

For some reason I was at their house particularly early one morning and was invited to sit with her and her children for a few moments of quiet before they went out the door for school. I don't remember exactly what she said to them, but I do remember she read from the Bible as a thought for the day and asked how she could pray for them. What a beautiful picture of how to be a godly mom. She helped her girls make God the first priority of their day, and didn't let them leave the house without knowing she carried their concerns, large and small, and that they were in her prayers. This became a pattern in my own mothering. Our time together before school as a family of boys rarely involved any stillness, but we did talk about God before school and I asked how I could pray for them. Daily we put on the armor of God from Ephesians 6, complete with the actions that went along with it. My boys loved to stomp their feet, and their brother's feet, as they recited the part of the verse that talked about feet fitted with the readiness to share the gospel of peace. The Sword of the Spirit, complete with a very dramatic sword thrust, was their favorite part. Thankfully the swords were imaginary or it could have been very dangerous. It didn't look the same in our house as it had in hers, but the principle was the same, point them to Jesus. My Southern sister taught me that.

When my first baby was born she gave me a baby shower. Our intimate group sat around her dining room table for lunch and then they prayed for us — Mike, me, and our little one. I had never been to a baby shower like it before. The gift she gave me was home-made. An Easter basket filled with decorated plastic eggs whose contents tell the story of Jesus' death and resurrection. I later used it to teach my children. What's left of it is now in the box of treasures I have saved for my grandchildren someday.

After two short years my road trip moved us away from Raleigh but, because of this friend, it still feels like home to me. She made room for me in her life when she had a young family and probably didn't have much room to spare. Without even realizing it, she pointed me to Christ. Likewise, Jesus was surrounded by crowds at all hours of the day and night and though He may have felt frustrated by their constant company it never showed. He just loved them. My Southern sister did that for me. She practiced so much more than Southern hospitality, which she did very well, she practiced godly hospitality.

My camp counselor friend taught me that God was knowable; my Southern sister taught me what it looked like when you live like you know Him. She poured out on others what she first took in herself, Jesus. I thought she was a role model for motherhood, but she was careful to point out that the model wasn't her, it was Jesus. She was a student of the Bible and used it as her handbook for marriage and parenting. She's also one of the most prayerful women I have ever met. I have moved several times and traveled widely since those days, but although remaining in Raleigh, she has traveled more than anyone I know — on her knees in prayer.

When we moved to Wisconsin she came to visit within a few months. We took her to the church we had just joined. It was much larger and very different from the congregation we had shared in Raleigh. In our walking around on Sunday morning we ran into the senior pastor whom we hardly knew. To our amazement, and probably because he loved her Southern accent, he offered to give us a tour of the new sanctuary currently under construction. For a busy man with a busy day, he invested the same kind of time and attention in us that she had invested in me. She wrote to him when she returned to Raleigh to tell him a few things about us, her friends who had just joined his church. That kind act opened doors for us to find intimate fellowship in a very large place and began a relationship with the church that would change our lives forever.

At the weddings of her daughters last year I was given a very special role, matron of honor to the mother-of-the-bride. We made that up. My job was to take the same kind of care of my friend that the official maid of honor did of the bride. What a privilege it was, and so much fun. I basically just followed her around for a week and did what she did, not much has changed!

I heard the weatherman say something so interesting on the news the other day. "There will be plenty of star shine in the sky tonight." Star shine, I had never thought of that. It must be the nighttime equivalent of sunshine. The Magi had one star that appeared to come and go. I've had a life filled with stars.

When our road trip took us to Wisconsin, after a brief stay in Cleveland, I thought my two small boys and I would freeze if we went outside, so we didn't, for weeks. Once we were settled, Mike hit the road again leaving me two choices, step out on my own or lose my mind. I decided to start with a Bible study. I didn't know the weather was treacherous that day and would never have thought to check. To me a lot of snow was pretty, not dangerous. I turned out to be one of only two people who braved a blizzard to get to church. That's how desperate I was to find warmth in this cold new environment; I chose the church because I didn't know where else to go.

Some stars shine from a distance, we don't see them up close or even know them well but they affect us deeply. I heard this star friend's voice before I officially met her. She led the teaching time at the Bible study. Her voice was warmth personified. The first time I had the chance to hear her speak at length was at a women's retreat called Breakaway. Her subject was Job and she spoke on suffering. I remember laughing a lot. Laughing during a message on suffering? I loved her right away. I have never seen anyone expand scripture with imagination the way she did. It was as if she looked into the actual hearts and minds of the Bible characters she unpacked and made the stories come alive from the inside out. It literally captured me. My camp counselor had taught me that God was knowable; my Southern sister had taught me that the Bible was livable, but this teacher friend taught me to look for more. She inspired me to look for more of God – the good part; more of myself – usually the bad part; and more application to my life – the transforming part. I have always been a copious note-taker, but I don't remember writing anything down that day – I was too busy listening, not to her, but to God. You could tell she knew Him well, He just poured out of her.

The first few times we crossed paths I re-introduced myself at each meeting. She was the senior pastor's wife and had so many people in her life I doubted she would remember me, but she did. The third time I spoke to her she said, "Oh I remember you," and we shook hands in the hallway. I'm not sure how we moved past a handshake but we did, maybe because she kept speaking and I kept listening. I read several of her books and learned she had said good-bye to her safety during the bombings of her wartime childhood. She said goodbye to her father, suddenly, and way too soon. She said goodbye to her husband's banking career and the comforts of it to join him in ministry. She said goodbye to her home country and the aging mother and beloved sister she had to leave behind to come to Wisconsin. Then she said goodbye to things here at home, her new home, to travel the world by her husband's side, teaching the Bible. She constantly said goodbye to women in one country so she could minister to women in another. Then she said goodbye to grandchildren — lots of them — as they grew and she traveled. To me that sounded like a lot of goodbye's for one woman. It made me sad for her until I remembered something, as a young woman in England years before, she had said hello to Jesus. He was what made the difference in her life. It didn't make things easy, but it did make them worth it.

We have become friends over the years and now embrace rather than shake hands. When she greets me she takes my face in her hands and calls me, "dear Elizabeth." I think she does that to lots of women, but it still feels special to me. I see Jesus in her gesture.

He knows each one of us intimately and despite the number of people on this earth, He treats us each as if we were the only one.

Despite her schedule, if I call her for coffee she will make it work, but I have to make it work too. I try to go to where she already is so she doesn't have to travel far to meet me. I have learned from watching her that she doesn't look for wide open spaces on her calendar, there are none, she looks for spaces that have just enough time. God can certainly bless just enough. Recently I asked her if she ever felt she deserved a break or even a blessing after a busy season of ministry. Her eyes welled up as she said in a very quiet voice, "No, I've never felt like what I did was enough and I am already so blessed." I saw a flash of starlight just then as she pointed me to Jesus, the one who made a sacrifice far greater than any I could even comprehend — for me — and asked nothing in return accept that I surrender my life to Him. He said goodbye to heaven so He could give up His rightful place as royalty and came to earth to live as a man, then suffered greatly only to say goodbye again to die in my place. She taught me what a surrendered life looks like, not hers but Jesus'. He sacrificed for me, who deserved nothing but the worst, so I could have the best, a life fully restored to God – how could I possibly feel he was somehow indebted to me?

Jesus knows us well, not just our beginning which we know, but our ending and everything in between. We can spend our lifetime trying to figure out what to do and how to do it, or we can ask Him, listen for His answers, watch for stars, and follow well. When we do this, every day begins with hello which makes the sting of goodbye much less.

Dark Stars

"Then Herod called the Magi secretly and found out from them the exact time the star had appeared."
Matthew 2:7

The star *had* appeared — past tense. To me that means they saw it in the East but they might not have seen it since. This still happens today. Sometimes the sky is dark and what I started out following is no longer in sight. It's not gone, just not easily visible at the moment.

As a child my dad worked for a big company that moved us many times. I am fortunate to have parents who've been married fifty-two years and three sisters I count among my dearest friends. There was an aspect of adventure to all this moving around that I truly loved, but it also meant being new, a lot, and often feeling like an outsider. After all these years, I finally have words to describe why it was hard for me. I have a high need to belong. I don't mean fitting in, that's different. I don't need to look like and act like everyone else, acceptance is not the issue. Rather it's a longing to be listened to and valued in a way that develops over time, into deep relationships. My parents and sisters offered that as I grew up, but I wanted roots and a history somewhere with people outside my family. When I married my native-Texan husband in 1984, I pictured a life in Houston, Texas where we lived at the time. I thought my children would grow up with my friend's children and we would live in the same town all our lives. I thought that's what I wanted and I got it, for about five years, but then we began to move. Mike worked for a large corporation similar to the one where my dad had worked for over thirty years. This lends itself to job security, but not to location security which mattered more to me. By 1992, we were well settled in Wisconsin and beginning to put down roots that would turn out to be deeper than any I had ever known. We had a house big enough for our four busy boys and a yard big enough to keep them a safe distance from the neighbors. For the safety of the neighbors, not the safety of the boys! We had friends who loved us like family and a church that both cared for and challenged us.

Mike knew his schedule wasn't ideal, but he didn't know exactly how to make a change until a friend and former co-worker offered him an opportunity to leave the big company, and the travel, and work with a smaller outfit. Unfortunately, it didn't go well and all the stars that had pointed us in that direction seemed to disappear. Within a year, we found his job security in jeopardy and our financial situation precarious as we went months without pay. The thought of moving again and leaving Wisconsin was difficult for me. I had roots here and the beginning of a history. I was very content at this rest stop in my road trip, but God had other plans. There were options for a job in Wisconsin, but the one Mike really wanted was back in Houston. I knew it was the right thing to do, but my heart literally broke as we decided, as much out of fear as out of sorrow

In my irrational mind I thought God was going to stay behind in Wisconsin and we would go forward without Him. I was afraid I couldn't be the new me in an old place and somehow convinced myself that my priorities were no longer the same as those of my old friends. I was afraid the God who had become so real and personal to me over the last ten years was finished with me. I had just begun to develop a passion for teaching the Bible and using the love I had for public speaking as a ministry to women. It felt like God had provided training, opportunity and a godly desire, then changed His mind and abandoned me. How sad that I gave God, and my friends, so little credit. Mike and I have often joked that we left Houston with two dogs and a Volvo and returned ten years later with four boys and a mini-van. I loved my old friends in Houston and looked forward to having our extended family just a few hours away, but I didn't want to go back. I knew I needed to look at things differently so I could see something different but I had lost my perspective.

When I could no longer see a really big star, I stopped looking up, began looking around and panicked. I let the world get in my way, in every way. I needed to be reminded that there was a star to start with when the guiding star was hard to see. It was time to look inside for a trusting star and just keep going. We'll look at how the Magi did this on their road trip in a later chapter.

We needed to sell our Wisconsin house in the dead of winter. When I mentioned this to a woman I knew from a small group she said, "We'll buy your house. I think it's just what we are looking for." They did. We needed to find a house in Houston and were concerned about where, in that giant city, and how much. I had not shared the possibility of a move with my friend Angela because she gets excited easily. I wasn't excited, I was sad, and the thought of her enthusiasm was more than I could handle. When we found out we might be moving back she called me immediately and started house hunting. At first I found her enthusiasm overwhelming, but it was contagious and my spirits began to lift. The house across the street from her was being renovated. She had never met the owner and there was no for sale sign in sight, but she went over right away and started asking questions. Her husband joked that she put up police tape, the yellow stuff that says "DO NOT CROSS," in bold letters, when she found out it was going up for sale so no one else could look at it before I did! It was the only house we looked at. We bought it right away.

Jerusalem too was a giant city for its day, probably very unlike the hometowns of the wise men, but they needed to stop there so they would be ready to continue their journey. Houston was like that for me. My old friend and new neighbor asked me before the boxes were even unpacked if I would do a Bible study with her and invite a few others. One who came was my friend Holly. Every time I moved, she visited. When I look at my life in pictures, I don't see places, I see Holly. I was shocked she wanted to come. The very thing I loved to do with women I dearly loved was right in front of me and I'd been in town less than a week. I was suddenly blinded by starlight. The God I thought had abandoned me had just relocated me and given me an opportunity I could never have imagined. In my mental picture of a ministry to women, it never looked this good. All I had learned about God being knowable, and the Bible being livable, and what a life surrendered to Jesus looked like poured out of me and on to these women and God multiplied it. The women wanted to include their husbands and neighbors so we did, and our house became a hub of activity every Sunday night with small groups meeting in the bedrooms. I remember the look on a friend's face when someone talked about the couples Bible study on Sunday nights that met in the Murphy's bedroom. It does sound rather odd. I was surprised every time I opened the door and saw my friend Keri with her husband who came for one of the studies. We had been friends since college, but our history together never predicted this particular future.

I was thriving in Houston loving my ministry, my family, and all things Texan but there were clouds on the horizon for my husband. His job was not going as expected and change became necessary. He was lower than I had ever seen him as we faced yet another move after only two short years. By this time we were genuinely despairing. We didn't want to start over in a new job situation, again; to uproot our children, again; or to leave our extended family, again. We both wondered aloud and often how something that seemed so promising had ended up so disappointing. On many days I just wandered around muttering the word trust. Craziness often comes with despair! I was looking for direction, but couldn't hear God say anything except trust me. It wasn't an audible voice I heard, but places in the Bible that I stumbled upon during my regular daily study and songs I was suddenly aware of on the radio where I heard His reassurance. I was beginning to look at things differently and seeing something different, an opportunity.

In his search for a new job, Mike made contact in Wisconsin with friends we knew from church. Business people like him. One, who happened to be the chairman of the elders at our old church, had a very unexpected response – he suggested Mike consider coming back to Wisconsin to the church as a pastor. I was not excited about this at all, but Mike was thrilled. Suddenly the night sky seemed filled with stars shining around his head, but it still looked dark to me. We knew this wasn't how God worked, dividing husbands and wives, and so we agreed to persevere together. We would discuss every detail and feeling no matter how hard to express or hear.

My engineering-minded husband had done a matrix of his goals for every area of his life and lined them up with all of the opportunities we were considering. In this, I saw a practical aspect of God I had never seen before. He knew Mike needed this kind of logical exercise, I however, respond better to artistic things like writing in the sky, which I asked for. The only position that lined up in every area of Mike's chart was the church. He took the matrix and presented it to seven men he trusted as friends, mentors, and brothers. All seven of them said, "Go for it." We had prayed that if we weren't supposed to do this that just one would say no. It's not a good idea to test God, but we do and He knows we will. It doesn't change anything, but it does make us feel better sometimes. After all that encouragement, I decided we needed a different prayer!

A wise older friend advised Mike to send me to Wisconsin by myself to talk to pastors and staff, and to seek God on my own. Those were very well-placed words of advice. I stayed with some long-time friends who had a history of loving us well, holding us accountable, and speaking God's truth into our lives. I met with eight different pastors and staff in one day and asked every question I could think of, even the ones that probably seemed embarrassing to my husband like, "What makes you think he can do this?" It sounded like I doubted Mike, or God, but I doubted myself. I knew my husband was a pastor at heart, but I was convinced I was not a pastor's wife and we certainly were not raising pastor's kids!

The heartfelt response to my question came from a pastor who knew Mike from serving with him during our previous time in Wisconsin. I don't remember exactly what he said, but it was something like, "I was there when Mike said goodbye to the elders as you left last time and I have rarely witnessed such a heartfelt parting. We've been praying he would come back since the minute he left." What? Come back? I was confused. In a detour the signs are often hard to follow and the change of course is frustrating. Houston suddenly felt like one of those frustrating detours but it ultimately did what detours do, it led us back to this right path by another route. It felt necessary.

When I got back to my friend's house that night I knew this was what a call from God looked like. It was a deep conviction that a road lay before us with a path clearly marked. To not follow would be to blatantly disobey God. My gracious hosts didn't even try to ask me about the day. I was out of words, which is rare for me. They settled me on the couch in front of the fireplace, served me dinner on a tray and left me alone to listen to God. I heard His voice in my heart saying the same thing He had been saying all along, trust me. We moved six short weeks later.

I grieved the losses of the Houston goodbyes for a long time and my friends and family grieved with me, moving away was the right thing to do. At the time it felt awful, but looking back I see God had a map in mind the whole time. There were curves and hills and what felt like dangerous places we had to pass through, but that's the point, we had to pass *through* them. We were shaped, stripped, and sometimes shattered on the road trip to this place, where we see God clearly, for now. Dark stars are like that. They don't cause celebrations here on earth, but they are cause for celebration in heaven because they ultimately point us toward Jesus and home.

Stars that Stay

"After they had heard the king, they went on their way, and the star they had seen in the east went ahead of them until it stopped over the place where the child was."
Matthew 2:9

Stars that stay are a curious phenomenon in astronomy. I don't understand the science, but I know there is something called retrograde motion that causes stars and planets to look as though they are standing still in the sky. That may be what happened over the house in Bethlehem where Mary and the young child Jesus were found, we don't know, but when a star comes in to my life and stays, I don't call it science, I call it God.

"...being confident of this, that he who began a good work
in you will carry it on to completion until the
day of Christ Jesus."
Philippians 1:6.

God doesn't just desire to start things in our lives
He desires to finish them. He wanted the Magi to go
the distance to Bethlehem, not to stop in Jerusalem and
to consider close good enough. I wonder how many
times they wanted to turn around and go home on their
long, long journey. Fear could have turned them back.
It must have been scary to meet with Herod, in secret,
and watch as he said one thing but plotted another.
These were learned men. I suspect they were suspi-
cious. Comfort could have kept them from continuing.
The palace had to be better than camping, if that's what
they had done along the way. They might have stayed
in the palace, because if Herod was going to keep their
meeting a secret he needed them to be nearby when he
called. They could have given into temptation and sold
the gifts they were carrying for Jesus to replenish their
supplies. That would be reason enough to give up. You
can't show up at a party, especially with this particular

guest of honor, empty handed. But they didn't, they persevered, and God sent back the star. We don't know that it had ever disappeared, but Scripture does keep saying, *had*.

One of the stars that has stayed in my life showed up when I was one year and eight days old, my younger sister Susan. We shared a room as children and even when my parents gave me my own room, I slept on the floor by her bed. I always started out in my own bed, but couldn't quite seem to make it through the night alone. We went to school together, went to camp together, and got our first job together. When we moved to Omaha, Nebraska, the summer before my senior year in high school, Susan and I navigated this new and unwelcome road together. Our older sister Amy, also very close in age, was going off to college and our youngest sister, Mary, was just in elementary school. It is said that misery loves company; Susan was all I had and I was miserable. You could say we bonded. I am close to all of my sisters, but there is just something about Susan.

When I was in college at Texas A&M University, I went through a strange phase where I thought I was a runner. I've always been clumsy and injury prone so it really was a bad idea, but I was determined. I trained with some friends and bravely, stupidly, entered a half marathon and Susan wanted to come down from school at Oklahoma State to watch. She was planning to be a nurse; I think she thought I might need one. My friends and I started out as a group, but they moved on quickly to keep up with the faster pace of the crowd. I don't remember anything about the weather; I don't remember being uncomfortable or that the race was hard, I just remember being alone, all alone. I noticed as the day wore on — a bad sign that this would take a whole day — that no one else was on the course. It was two loops around campus so at about the halfway point you passed near what would be the finish line.

When I passed I saw crowds with balloons and streamers and lots of big banners. It looked like a very enthusiastic and welcoming place. I couldn't wait until my turn to cross. Hours later when I was within sight of it again all I saw was one man, a van with the doors open, and Susan. This seemed odd until I noticed the friends I had started with gathered a distance away, already showered, changed, and eating. To my horror,

I realized I was literally the last person on the course, and I had been for a long time.

The race banner was gone, the streamers and balloons were gone, and the enthusiastic crowd of hours before had dwindled to a crowd of one, my sister. I didn't count the man with the van because I found out later he had wanted to leave for a long time but couldn't because they had to account for every runner who started and he was responsible for the equipment. Susan literally begged him to keep the course open until I finished instead of counting me as a drop- out. No wonder he looked so unhappy. It makes me cry to recall, all these years later, how she was jumping up and down and screaming like I was the winner instead of her worn-out sister who finished last. She didn't care that I nearly crawled across what used to be the finish line, gone remember. She just stayed until I finished.

God does that. He knows how prepared or unprepared you are for what lies ahead. He knows where the hard parts are and the kind of support you will need to get through them. He will meet you where you are, carry you along the way, and stay, until you find Him, like the Magi did.

What happened in the sky at the time of Jesus' birth was an unexplainable phenomenon. It simply defies description. My whole life is like that. I have found peace where there should have been none, guidance given to me personally by the Creator of the Universe, and blessings I did not deserve. I have been given friends who love and support me, a family I adore and most days adores me, and adventures that God alone could orchestrate. There have been, and will be, hard parts but they are purposeful and if I look at them differently, as detours on my road trip home, I will see something different and there will be joy. As I studied Matthew, chapter 2, my goal was to have some new insights about Christmas. I have, but it's been so much more than that, it's been a chance to look back with a new view and revisit my own journey toward Jesus. The star sightings, dark stars, and stars that stay are all part of what God used in my life. What has he used in yours? I challenge you to stop here and use the questions on the following page to recall your own road trip – then pack your bags – the road awaits.

Keep Traveling
Chapter 2 - Discovering a Star
While Gazing at the Moon

1. God is infinitely practical using the people and experiences in our everyday lives to point us to Him, but we will miss it if we don't pay attention. What distracts you and keeps you from paying attention to Him?

2. Make a list of the "stars" in your life who have pointed you toward Christ?
   (Do not dismiss anything as a circumstance and be creative.)

3. Beside each name write down what you learned from him or her. It probably won't be something they intentionally taught you, but rather, something about how they lived and how they loved you that pointed you to Jesus. Write a note to someone on your list letting him or her know the impact he or she has had on your life.

4. Encouragement is particularly important when the sky seems dark. What encourages you in dark times? (I read old journals or notes I have written in my Bible that remind me of God's faithfulness in the past. It helps me to remember when I write things down. I re-memorize Scriptures that were meaningful in dark times, but I've since forgotten.) If now is a dark time, write down your thoughts at this moment. Be honest and write down all the reasons you want to stop traveling this journey you're on and just go home. Then write down all the reasons you should persevere and a list of things you can do to help you along the way. The Magi talked to friends, they prayed, they kept looking up.

5. Think about the stars that have stayed in your life. It's easy to stop seeing their unique brightness when they are consistently part of your night sky. Don't let their presence go unnoticed or unappreciated. Thank them, and thank God for their faithfulness.

Chapter 3

A Roaring Ruler
Herod

I heard a story once about the hunting habits of African lions; it reminded me of King Herod. The young lions in the family group are strong, agile, fast, and fearless. They are also constantly hungry. They travel in a pack, called a pride, on an endless search for food. This sounds a lot like the teenage boys I see around my dinner table every night!

As a lion ages he loses his speed, his strength, his teeth, but never his appetite. The last thing to go is his roar. Lions have the loudest roar of all the big cats. The sound can be heard from as far away as five miles. Once the pride selects their prey, usually a herd rather than a single animal, they take up positions and attack as a group with each playing a specific role. The roles change over time. The oldest lion is placed on the far side of the hunted, opposite the younger stronger lions. Where he once led the pack, his job now has become to stay in the shadows and roar as loud as he can scaring the hunted animals away from the thing they think they fear and toward the thing they should fear, the jaws of the hungry pride. The old lion has no real power left but to scare the prey. That's all he can do. After all the younger lions have had their fill of food, the old lion is left to feast on what's left — scraps are hard to reach when you are practically toothless. The old lion still has a certain degree of power in that he *appears* dangerous. He's still scary and his roar allows him to continue manipulating others. The problem is that he doesn't get much to eat leaving him empty and dissatisfied most of the time.

I believe this is a picture of King Herod when we meet him in Matthew, chapter 2. He is an old man in poor health still hungry for power and roaring like crazy to maintain control.

Herod's History

Lions are known as the king of beasts; Herod was just a beastly king. At the time of Jesus' birth, Herod the Great, as he was known, was probably in his late sixties, nearing the end of his reign and fatally ill. A history of his life said, at this point, he suffered from several miserable diseases including chronic itching and had very few people around him that he trusted. In a jealous rage over family rivalries, Herod had put to death the two sons of his Jewish second wife Mariamne, Mariamne herself, her brother, sister, mother, and grandfather along with Antipater, his son from his first wife and once heir to the throne. As he became more and more paranoid and delusional it is said that he wandered the halls of his palace calling out for Mariamne, whom he truly loved. Isolated and itching, it sounds awful.

His journey to the throne did not begin in his own family; he was appointed King of Judea rather than born to it. He was only half Jewish and a commoner which made him very unpopular with the people he ruled. His marriage to Mariamne, who was from a prominent Jewish family, was an effort on his part to gain the good graces of the Jews in his kingdom, but that too had failed miserably. As he grew older he married new women – ten in all – trying to ease his loneliness. He took special baths trying to soothe his physical discomfort and traveled extensively and expensively trying to find new distractions, but nothing satisfied. Then the Magi from the East showed up talking about a star and one who was born king of the Jews. It must have threatened Herod on every level. He would have seen any king, especially this long-awaited one, as a genuine rival to his power and authority.

God used the star the Magi saw in the East to turn them into travelers on a journey toward Jesus and into troublemakers in the eyes of King Herod. They were stars in his life, pointing him toward the King of Kings, but instead of following a leading light he mistakenly anticipated a dangerous darkness. When you look at things differently you will see something different. Herod didn't like what he saw.

Herod's Heart

I think Herod was a man with a broken heart. He started out with great promise and a genuine desire to lead well but his road trip did not lead him anywhere he intended. His life was like a roller coaster ride. In the beginning there was nowhere to go but up. As the car climbed higher and the view got better there was an exhilarating sense of power and control; then the bottom fell out. As the car descended faster and faster the sense of powerlessness became overwhelming. Herod made one bad choice and mistake after another and instead of learning from them, he made more. The ride went on and on, up and down because he would not let anyone throw the switch and stop the car. Herod would have to surrender to a power other than his own if the cycle of control was going to stop. The world of politics that had so inspired him instead disappointed him. In an effort to please everyone, he pleased no one. Instead of ruling others, he became ruled by his own anxiety and fear.

Interestingly, he was called the prince of peace but the only kind he experienced was the uneasy kind. Peace that was dependent upon everything in his world going according to his plan with him at the center of it, in control. He wanted to be at peace with his people, with his family, and in his body, and would do anything including committing murder and creating mayhem to make that happen. That's where anxiety leads, to an overwhelming need to control. Herod became a control freak.

I know it seems trivial, but I experience this when I have stayed up late doing load after load of laundry — boys are a dirty business and I stand in awe before the clear bottom of an empty laundry chute. Peace descends, for a moment, and then a sock arrives. Just one sock, the other has vanished never to be seen again. I feel this same uneasy peace again when the kitchen is clean at the end of a long day and then while my back is turned and someone quickly puts a bowl of cereal milk in the sink. Everything in *my* narrow little world is not going according to *my* plan and I am not at the center of it. On days like these I am all about power and control – mine!

I wish it were just laundry and dishes, but it's so much more than that. I have never committed murder or caused the kind of mayhem Herod did, but I've killed the joy in my children when I have roared at them over behavior that embarrasses me. Not bad behavior, but behavior I don't like. I have caused mayhem in our family finances when I have selfishly spent beyond our means and then lied to my husband to cover my sin. I have damaged my own extended family relationships with angry impatient words, a judgmental attitude, and selfish behavior. Compared to Herod, I am not so bad but compared to Jesus — I am speechless with despair. It is at times like these that I realize I have a heart like Herod's. I am broken by my sin and the choices I make every day that dismiss God in my life. Like Herod, I cling too tightly to control, letting small things distract me from the God who created me, who loves me, and who died for me. He alone offers lasting peace, the kind that has nothing to do with my control but everything to do with His.

Dictionary.com says control means, "To have dominion over, to manage, govern and have authority over." It looks like someone who doesn't trust others, who needs to do most things herself, who is concerned about every small detail, who is easily irritated, and who doesn't take it lightly when others disagree with her, ignoring her advice. Control looks like Herod and often a lot like me.

Matthew 2:3 says, "When King Herod heard this he was disturbed, and all Jerusalem with him." I can see why Jerusalem would be disturbed. Herod was a disturbing guy and when he felt threatened he did very disturbing things. The people of his kingdom, especially those in his inner circle, had become a people used to treading lightly for fear of upsetting him. Experience had taught them that pleasing Herod was important, their lives depended on it, and he was very hard to please. Godly kings are remembered well; children are often even named in their honor. However, I've never met a boy named Herod.

Herod's heart scares me, because it looks so much like mine. I, too, can struggle with the notion of submitting my will to the will of someone else. It can be in small things like the way I drive, or run my home, to big things like respecting the thoughts and opinions of other people. I want to determine how and where to invest my time, talent, and treasure (money) and where I look for guidance and counsel — so did

Herod. God created each of us, including Herod, in His image. That means He wants us to look to Him so we can look more like Him. When control is my problem I look around and not up, to what my friends and family members think and say, what culture commands, and what will please me. The more I do this, the more I start to look like the world around me and the less I look like Jesus. The world around me is full of fear and anxiety. Kindness is the exception rather than the norm and pride is praised over humility and sacrifice. In the world we live in love does not last and truth is relative. Jesus is about so much more than that and wants so much more for me.

The word *submit*, as it is used in the Bible in reference to submitting my will to the will of God, is actually a military term that means "to assume the proper rank. To stand in the right position based on the training and equipment you have and allow others to assume their proper rank."

I see very little compared to what God sees. He is omniscient which means He sees all, past, present, and future, all people in all places all the time. There is no equipment He needs and no experience He doesn't know or understand. Jesus suffered throughout life on earth and death on a cross, partly so we could know we have someone to put our trust in who has truly walked where we walk and lived what we live.

I know several young people who are just beginning their careers in the military. It's exciting for them and impressive for me to hear about the training they receive. Each new assignment involves intense time spent learning what they need to know and then practicing what they've learned. The higher the rank, the more training and experience they receive. I will never have to go into battle with them but, if I did, I would happily take my place behind them trusting that they know best, that they have the right equipment for the job, and that they will use their experience to care for those in their command, especially me. I think I would confidently follow their lead. I have no problem giving every piece of important information to someone who is good with computers and to willingly submit my body to the care of a doctor, who is well trained to do what he does, but behave so often as if God is inadequate. I become so distracted by the exhilaration of the ascent that I forget a frightening descent lies just around the next bend in the track of the roller coaster. The first step toward any real change is admitting my powerlessness and recognizing that any control I have is nothing more than a hoax.

Herod's Hoax

"When he had called together all the people's chief priests and teachers of the law, he asked them where the Christ was to be born" (Matthew 2:4). I looked up this verse in five different translations of the Bible. The word that was common to every version was, "all." Herod was both determined and thorough; he called together ALL the chief priests and teachers of the law. He wanted to know the exact time the star had appeared and he wanted a careful search to take place. He called the priests of the people — those from the city — so he would know what was being said in the streets. He cared desperately about what others thought. He was also afraid. Fear brings out our worst insecurities and causes us to see everyone as competition. We start to look for loopholes, ways to discredit others and opportunities to manipulate things to go our way. I think Herod needed as much information from as many sources as possible so he could be sure he wasn't missing anything and stay in control.

When I feel out of control, I so often forget the big picture, getting caught up in the small stuff. I lose sight of God's grand scope and shrink the view down to what matters to me. I see this in the raising of my children. The daily hard work of being a parent and the drama that goes with it often sidetracks me. It's then that I can forget others like youth leaders and teachers who are also working hard on behalf of my children. My children are God's children not mine and they are on their own journey to becoming really amazing adults. So often I get distracted by long hair and dirty bedrooms and don't look at their hearts that I am so proud of and the character that God is ultimately shaping in them. This also happens when I plan a party or event. I get so consumed with the details of the food and decorations, I forget that people are coming — the gathering is intended to bless them, not showcase me. This happens in church when we pretend to worship, paying more attention to *who* is preaching the sermon rather than the God of the sermon. When people become a problem and not our purpose, when worship becomes all about what we get and not about who God is, then we have a problem. It's as if we lose our map and the destination, Jesus, only becomes a detour on the way to glorifying ourselves. Soon, our Herod hearts start beating outside our bodies for all to see.

God has made it very clear in His Word that this is *His* world. He is in charge and we are to adore Him for that. Adore. I don't want to adore Him for being in charge; I want to be in charge. As I write this I feel the beating of a Herod heart in my chest and must come face-to-face with the danger of worshiping the wrong king, myself.

Me, me, me, it seemed to be a theme song for Herod. He told the Magi that he too wanted to worship Jesus. He too, as in also. The Magi were very clear about the purpose of their visit which must have frightened Herod out of his mind, literally. Rather than think through his options, he acted quickly. Matthew 2:3-4 in The Message says, "Herod lost no time." The same verses in the Amplified Bible say, "...he anxiously asked them where the Christ was to be born." He had a history of impulsive behavior followed quickly by regret. People with control issues often do, as soon as we have just enough information, we move forward. What looks like enthusiasm is actually panic. We need to act before someone else does. We think it shows decisiveness and looks like leadership. God doesn't move that way. His leadership is timeless and trustworthy. For thousands of years leaders have come and gone, but Christ remains. He truly does have all the information and when we seek Him, He will guide us, at the right pace to the right place. His desire to have dominion over our lives comes from His love for us and the fullest understanding of what is best for us. God does say Me, Me, Me but not for the same selfish reason that Herod did. He knows that only by looking to Him will we find our best selves and the peace we long for.

Herod's next move after the Magi mission failed was to murder all of the boy children Jesus' age. If he couldn't kill the one he wanted, he would kill them all. Even in the face of great failure he clung to his illusion of control and died a paranoid and delusional old man. It was a heartbreaking end for this heartbroken man who chose to stay on a roller-coaster ride and never completed his journey toward Jesus.

Herod's Hope

Things could have ended so differently for Herod, but they didn't. There is always hope, no matter what we've done. Jesus never gives up on us — any of us. I love that the star in Matthew 2 is called, "his" star and that it stayed. It is a picture of the faithfulness of the God who keeps reaching out to us even as we turn our backs on Him.

For some of us this idea of submission is new and frightening. The idea of a God who chooses to pursue rather than be pursued is hard to grasp. I wonder what picture came to mind for the people of Herod's day when they imagined this new King, Jesus. Herod, as their model of kingship was a beast and a bad guy; Jesus was neither, yet they may have viewed Him through their own bad king experience. Others may have seen the heavenly Father in the image of their own earthly fathers and the picture was not comforting. God is like no king and no man ever known; He is entirely different.

Instead of a lion, He is a lamb. In the familiar words of 1 Corinthians 13: 4-7, "Love is patient, love is kind. It does not envy, it does not boast, it is not proud. It is not rude, it is not self-seeking, it is not easily angered, it keeps no record of wrongs. Love does not delight in evil but rejoices with the truth. It always protects, always trusts, always hopes, always perseveres." Put the word Jesus in the place of the word love and you will have a picture of Jesus, the One who asks for the surrender of your life. He is the One who says in Matthew 11:28-30, "Come to me, all you who are weary and burdened, and I will give you rest. Take my yoke upon you and learn from me, for I am gentle and humble in heart, and you will find rest for your souls. For my yoke is easy and my burden is light." When I read those words I think of Herod the roaring ruler, incredibly weary and burdened, who tried in his own power to find rest for his soul. He never grasped that surrendering to the very king he feared was the only way to find it. Surrender is scary, especially when it means letting go of the things we hold most dear.

When my children were small they would do what I told them, for the most part. If not, a word of correction or a well-placed swat on the rear end would solve the problem. I knew what was best for them and could usually get their cooperation as I enforced my will upon them. This illusion of control continued until they became teenagers. My oldest son wanted a tattoo to honor the grandfather he was very close to. We discussed it with him and gave him many reasons why we thought this was a bad idea. He listened politely, did not argue, and quietly went on his way—a few weeks after he turned eighteen he came home and proudly showed me the fresh ink on his upper, inner arm. "Please tell me that is a Sharpie drawing," I replied. When he told me it wasn't, I burst into tears. He quickly replied, "Don't worry mom it didn't hurt at all." I wasn't worried about his hurt, I was worried about mine. Truly, for the first time in our 18-year relationship with our son he had listened to our input and chosen to disregard it. He was not disrespectful or rude; he just made up his own mind. This really bothers control freaks. His choice wasn't life-altering or life-threatening, but it changed my view of his life — I had lost control. I had to come to terms with the fact that his choices are going to be different from the choices I would make for him. His life will have ups and downs I cannot smooth out for him and the consequences will be his to suffer. I was forced to recognize that my control over his life was an illusion and it had crumbled. It sounds dramatic, tattoos are very common these days, but in my world it was big. It changed the relationship I have with my oldest child. I had to step aside and surrender my son to the only One who has any control to begin with, Jesus. He knows the past, present, and future of my child far better than I ever will. God's control comes out of His desire to be our provider, our protector, and our promise keeper and is motivated by a love so deep we cannot begin to grasp its depth.

This kind of God and this kind of love are a hard concept to grasp for young people from broken families who wonder if there is any such thing as a love that lasts. They feel betrayed and out of control in their world because no one seems to be standing firm in the center of it. I was driving one of my older boys back to school and had to share with him the hard news that a beloved relative was getting a divorce. After I told him, he was quiet for a long time. When he finally spoke it was to ask, "Who will get custody of the kids?" "They are all adults," I replied, "no one has custody of you once you turn 18." After a few more minutes of silence he said with a quiver in his deep manly voice, "Mom, no matter how old I am, I will always need to know who has custody of me." This is the cry of every heart. We all want to know someone is in charge, someone has our best interest at heart, and that we *matter* to someone. When we surrender control to Jesus, we become children of the King, and custody is settled for all of eternity. John 10:27-28 says, "My sheep listen to my voice; I know them and they follow me. I give them eternal life, and they shall never perish; no one can snatch them out of my hand." In our Herod hearts we run from relationship to relationship looking for someone else to do for us what only God can, complete us. "Now to him who is able to do immeasurably more than all we ask or imagine, according to his power that is at work within us...," (Ephesians 3:20). This is the God who is asking us to surrender our will, to His. He wants our best, His way. When we run from relationship to relationship and find ourselves alone, again, finally looking to Jesus, we will find Him and understand that He is the God who stays. He is waiting to be found by those who seek Him. He sees your Herod heart and reaches out to you with the hope Herod missed, the hope of Jesus. "We who have run for our very lives to God have every reason to grab the promised *hope* with both hands and never let go. It's an unbreakable spiritual lifeline, reaching past all appearances right to the very presence of God where Jesus, running on ahead of us, has taken up his permanent post as high priest for us, in the order of Melchizedek, " (Hebrews 6:19, The Message – italics mine).

My status as a child of God became secure the moment I began my relationship with Christ through a simple prayer. My peace in that status changes daily, sometimes hourly, as I continue to fight for control. It's a moment-by-moment surrender that will be a challenge for the rest of my life. I know this, but I often don't live as if I do when it comes to many of the decisions I make. I don't even consult God, or I make a choice and then ask God to bless the decision I've made. How foolish of me. I can't even breathe without the second-by-second involvement of God in my life. "The God who made the world and everything in it is the Lord of heaven and earth and does not live in temples built by hands. And he is not served by human hands, as if he needed anything, because he himself gives all men life and breath and everything else" (Acts 17:24-25). When I hold my breath or something holds it for me, I become desperate to the point of choking and I gasp. The same desperation I feel at being kept from breath is the same desperation I should feel when I choose to keep myself from Jesus. When I come to my senses and come back to Christ, I do gasp. For Him, and the freshness that comes from surrendering, yet again, control. The roller coaster comes to a stop. The bar lifts off my lap. Peaceful quiet replaces the rumbling on the tracks and in my heart and I hear a voice saying, "exit carefully and safely," and I can because of Christ.

Keep Traveling
Chapter 3 - A Roaring Ruler

1. How do you see Herod differently now that you've read more about him?

2. How do you see yourself differently? Perhaps you've had a glimpse of your own Herod heart.

3. Herod's fear, paranoia, and need to control cost him his beloved wife Mariamne, several of his children, the respect of the citizens in his kingdom, and a trusting working relationship with his superiors in Rome. What has your need to control cost you?

4. How do you feel about the word *submit*? Does it make you feel powerless? That could be because you are—you can't breathe, walk, see, or hear without God's involvement in your life. How does this make you feel?

5. Make a list of your top ten worries — the things that preoccupy your heart and mind. Next to each item write down what you can *actually* do to impact the problem. If there is something you can do, do it. Then let go of the rest and leave them to God; there is no other choice.

6. What scares you about the idea of surrendering control?

7. What holds you back? List every reason you have for not trusting Christ as you live out the faith you have.

Herod did one thing right in Matthew, chapter 2. He went to those with answers to ask his questions. In his case this was the chief priests and teachers of the law. In our case, it's God. God has answers to your questions. Prayerfully present Him with the lists you have just made and ask for help with your concerns. Read the Bible for additional answers.

Many Bibles have a topical index in the back. It is a great place to start when you want to see what Scripture says on a specific subject. Your concerns are not new; many will be listed in this type of index.

8. In your heart, do you believe Jesus can be trusted? Why or why not?

Chapter 4

Heartless Head Men
The Chief Priests and Teachers of the Law

My three older sons are skateboarders. If they aren't skating they are watching skateboarding videos on the computer and planning tricks to try the next time they film a video of their own. I listened to them from the other room as they talked about a skater they were watching in a competition on TV. The boy was doing really well but they weren't cheering for him, they called him a poser. When I asked what that meant, they said it means he is in it for the money, not for the love of the sport. It turns out he was good at lots of other sports before he landed in skateboarding so it wasn't his first love. There is no respect for second place affection in skateboarding. You are either all in, or you are not. Posers are also those who wear the clothes and shoes, but don't ride the board. The boys really don't like posers. They get close to the sport without participating — all glory, and no guts.

Posers

The chief priests in Matthew 2 were religious leaders whose business it was to study and explain the Old Testament and instruct the people. The teachers of the law were lawyers in charge of the civil and religious affairs of the Jews. They appeared very devout but, sadly, were not very devoted. They were posers like the boy in the skateboard competition. Jesus was second in their affection; their first love was the law.

If you followed it to the letter, you were okay. If not, you were in trouble – no grace, no heart. The law was the standard by which all men were judged. Its purpose in the Old Testament was to show men their shortcomings. When you fell short, it was impossible not to, sacrifices had to be made to atone for sin and restore a right standing before God. The law was very black and white, very clear cut, very definitive. I think they were comfortable with that. Too comfortable. They missed what Jesus offered, the spirit of the law filled with limitless love and unending grace, focusing instead on the rules.

In the very orderly orthodox world of the chief priests and teachers, the law was a to-do list. As long as they could follow along and keep checking things off, they thought they had no problem. What they had; however, was an impossible problem. Who makes the list? Who decides when to check things off? Who decides the value of the work and the standard by which we are measured? When we make our own list, which is what we do with the law, then we put ourselves in charge. We decide when enough is enough. It reminds me of driving through a roundabout.

The city where I live has just completed one of these near my home. It intimidates me because I know how to get in, but I don't always know how to get out. I end up going around several times because I don't trust myself to decide the right time to exit. *I don't trust myself,* that's the problem. I hesitate at every opportunity to exit and ask myself, "Is this right? Have I gone far enough?" Then I keep going, around and around.

It's a frustrating way to drive and an exhausting way to live. We don't get to decide because nothing we can do on our own, through a list or a law will ever be enough. If I cannot be trusted with when to exit a roundabout in a relatively quiet area of town, how can I possibly be trusted to decide what will be enough to earn me the grace of God? Driving around in circles for a lifetime, never quite sure when it's time to exit is not the abundant life Jesus offers. It would be impossible to rest, ever, if this were the plan. With Jesus' plan there is no list, no record of wrongs to make up for. Nothing I can do on my own, through a list or a law will ever be enough because the law was all about what we should do, but couldn't; Jesus is all about what *He* would do, and did. It's impossible to please God without faith and faith is…"being sure of what we hope for and certain of what we do not see" (Hebrews 11:1). The Message calls faith, "our handle on what we can't see." It has to do with the heart, what you *believe*, not the head, what you *know*.

The Magi started their road trip when Herod anxiously summoned them to the palace and asked them about Jesus. It ended there too. Bethlehem was six short miles away, but the chief priests and teachers of the law didn't go. These religious leaders could have acted as escorts for the Magi, even if they went out of simple curiosity. But they didn't, they stayed in Jerusalem and drove around in circles, satisfied that their own efforts were enough and trusting themselves. They got so close to the One who would change everything, but they didn't participate. Posers, all glory, but no guts. It takes moving out of your comfort zone to go the distance to Jesus. It takes getting out of the roundabout and trusting in the work He has done on your behalf. Just take a few small steps in His direction; He will do the rest.

I love stories, particularly about people, those I know well and those I've never met. The stories of people are also my favorite in the Bible. I read biographies and watch the biography channel. I'm also secretly addicted to the storytelling news programs on television that share the lives of both the celebrities and the uncelebrated. I admit I read *People* magazine from time to time. The sports channels have profiles of athletes who have achieved success at every level and those who have squandered their potential. I am fascinated. Those who have come out of hardship or overcome their failures almost always speak of their faith; there's a reason for that. They've gone the distance. Those who are at the top of their world also say something common to both. They ask, "Is this all there is?" They may not use those exact words, but it's at the heart of what they are saying. The answer is *no*. Bethlehem is just a few short miles away, but the chief priests and teachers of the law are stuck where they are, unable or unwilling to move toward Jesus. It's easy to keep Christ at a distance because of wrong conclusions, poor information, religious upbringing, or the conflicted behavior of others, but Christ longs to get to know you in a deeply personal way. A relationship with Christ will change your life forever in a way that nothing else can. Why settle for anything less? I heard a woman in church one Sunday say she had reservations about becoming a Christian because she thought Christians were dull and they only wore brown and gray. She liked makeup and bright colors. If she had looked at Scripture she would have met some of the women who followed Jesus. She would have discovered that He was surrounded by women of all kinds, some who were wealthy and very well-dressed, others in desperate circumstances and dressed to match. The outside never mattered to Him.

I personally love red — clothes, nails, and lipstick – anything red. I hardly own any brown or gray, but if I did it wouldn't matter. My Christian friends are the most delightful free-spirited friends I have. They are exciting to be around because they are not ruled by insecurities, because they are secure in their relationship with Christ. They are free from the bondage of perfectionism, because they realize Jesus was the only perfect person and He doesn't expect perfection from us, just progress. These women are well-read and smart so the conversation is stimulating and thought-provoking. Some are divorced, some are single, and others are both happily and unhappily married. We shop, we eat, we decorate, and we diet. We complain about our husbands, our waistlines, and our frown lines. Our children both delight and disappoint us. We laugh louder and cry harder than any group of women I have ever known. For the woman who thinks she would lose out on life and fun by becoming a Christian, I say you have no idea what you are missing. The Christian women I have in my life give me something so unique — unconditional love with great accountability. I am allowed to be angry and frustrated and to have a bad day without being judged for it. They ask questions that help me to see things from different perspectives and challenge my behavior in ways that lead me to take responsibility for my part and forgive others for theirs. I've heard it described as "the kind truth." That is what my Christian friends tell me. Then we move forward. They pray for me and I pray for them. No request is too large or too small. They receive my successes with celebration and my failures with compassion. It is the best kind of friendship because it is real and deep and based on the unshakeable foundation of a relationship with Christ. It is a joy to be a follower of Christ in the midst of such women.

I meet others who won't go the distance to Jesus because they are content where they are. They're successful and comfortable and happy. To them, a life lived for Jesus sounds unattractive because it can mean suffering. What they don't realize is that, at some point in all of our lives, things will get hard and be filled with suffering — with or without Jesus. If it's not today, it will be some day. God doesn't cause suffering, sin does, our own sin or the sins of others that spill into our lives. I have two friends who have lost young adult sons in the last five years, both as the result of car accidents completely out of their control. One was killed by a drunk driver as he left a high school basketball game, the other was traveling with an adult driver and a group of friends back to his college campus when a truck driver fell asleep and crossed the median.

Accidents happen to those who follow Jesus and those who don't. Illness happens to Christians and non-Christians alike. When a tragedy occurs, people often say, "I don't deserve this." Does that mean we deserve the good that happens to us, but not the bad? I don't think so. We are created in the image of God because we're given the free will to make our own choices. Because we aren't God this image becomes scarred by sin. In a world full of sinful people each making their own selfish choices, things often go badly. The difference is that those who follow Jesus suffer with purpose. Romans 5:1-5 says, "Therefore, since we have been justified through faith, we have peace with God through our Lord Jesus Christ, through whom we have gained access by faith into this grace in which we now stand. And we rejoice in the hope of the glory of God. Not only so, but we also rejoice in our sufferings, because we know that suffering produces perseverance; perseverance, character; and character hope. And hope does not disappoint us, because God has poured out his love into our hearts by the Holy Spirit, whom he has given us." Christians grieve and mourn in the same way as everyone else, but with hope and the trust that God will take their suffering and use it for His ultimate good. We don't always know what that good is at the time, but God does and His plans will never be thwarted. As I've said before, *when you look at things differently you will see something different.* Believers look for Christ in their suffering and they find Him along with a peace that cannot be grasped until it grasps them. There is the comfort of everlasting arms that are present when no earthly arms are and the assurance of Heaven where there will be no more tears.

At the funeral of my friend's son, I stood next to her as we sang. I wept as she wept and then I noticed her hand extended out to her side and open, palm up. It was as if she was saying to God, "I don't want this, but

I will receive it if You will stand with me and hold me up and use it." It has been difficult, lonely, and desperately sad, but Christ has been there standing with her, holding her up. There have been feelings of anger and confusion, but I have seen, up close, the good that has come from it. When a follower of Jesus says, "I am mad at God," people are shocked, but God is not. He knows and understands our every feeling and is anxious for us to bring them to Him, in prayer, so He can walk us through them.

Recently a young man I met talked about a dream he had on and off for years. His journey toward Jesus had taken him down many broken roads, some he chose some he didn't. He took every detour possible often into dangerous places like drugs and alcohol and he raged with anger. Throughout his travels, he dreamed he was in a small room with no door. Every surface including the floor and the low ceiling were covered with several inches of tar – it was hot and dark, smelly and foreboding. In this dream he was always alone in the room. When he finally reached the end of himself and his efforts to soothe his hurt and deal with his anger, he came to Jesus and raged at Him. In our brief meeting, he told my husband and me about shaking his fist at God and screaming at Him. God welcomes this kind of brutal honesty. It's not the kind of prayer you hear in church or in small groups, because it's too personal for that, but it's the kind of prayer that comes from the deepest hurts that only God alone can heal. No one else can see our lives in their entirety with a full understanding of all we've experienced and how we've felt. Jesus can't help us move toward Him until we allow Him to move us past our past. This young man did that. He raged and ranted, then he confessed and accepted and went the distance. He had the dream again a while later only this time he wasn't alone in the room. Jesus was there and asked him, "What do you want me to do for you?" He woke up at that point and pondered the answer for days. Finally in prayer he was able to say to Jesus, "I don't know what I want, but I know that this room hasn't changed. It is better in here and I am okay because You are in it with me." I don't think he's had the dream since. Life is hard for everyone and suffering comes to everyone, eventually. The unstable foundation of success and happiness will

not hold up when it does. Jesus alone makes the difference and with Him we are never alone.

Many women feel alone and have trouble trusting
because they've been deeply wounded. They struggle
to put their faith in anyone, even those who know and
love them best. They have felt exposed and unprotected
in life and wondered, especially as children, who was
caring for them. They have bad examples of care and
picture the faces of those who have hurt them when
they picture Christ. This grieves God's heart terribly.
He has so much He wants for their lives. Our past will
have power only as long as we allow it to. Jesus wants
to reframe our past and restore our hope in the future,
but He will not force it. We must go the distance, just
a few small steps at a time, and choose to accept the
promise God has made to make us new creations.
"Therefore, if anyone is in Christ, he is a new creation;
the old has gone, the new has come!" (2 Corinthians
5:17).

The chief priests and teachers of the law settled
for less. Knowing about Jesus, but sadly, never really
knowing Him. Hopefully you don't make that same
mistake. A religious history is a good thing, but it is

often the very thing that has left you misinformed about your need for a relationship with Christ. You are told that living a "good life" is all that matters so you spend your effort and energy trying to do more good than bad and find yourself dizzy in the roundabout trying to keep track. Don't stay in Jerusalem, or wherever you are, dare to go the distance to Jesus. Make room for Him. Allow Him to be who He promises to be in your life. Discover Him for yourself by asking Him every question that comes to your mind. Pray through your doubts and give your concerns to God. Answers for your journey can be found in the Bible. Look for yourself and see how Jesus responds to the people He meets. As you get to know Christ personally, you will see your sin and as a result, your need. The first step in moving toward Jesus as your Savior is acknowledging your need for one. The closer you move toward Jesus, the closer He will move toward you. The Frenchman Blaise Pascal said it well, "I would rather live as if God exists to find out that He doesn't than live as if He doesn't exist to find out He does."

Performers

In my imagination one reason the chief priests and teachers of the law didn't continue on to Bethlehem is because they were too busy. They handled the sacrifices, teaching, and serving at the temple every time the doors were open. They had a specific wardrobe that needed careful tending and the ongoing ritual of cleansing. They had public prayer, private prayer and people were everywhere. I'm not dismissing the importance of their obligations, just pointing out that it sounds like they were busy, busy, busy. I wonder if they consulted the Scriptures as much as they did their calendars as they lived out their devotion to God. I wonder what those watching thought of them. I wonder what they think of me.

I had a neighbor when my children were small that I desperately wanted to reach with the love of Jesus. I invited her to every event at my church, to Bible studies, and activities for her children. I looked for opportunities to talk to her about spiritual things and tried to connect her to other Christians. We both had traveling husbands and found dinner time lonely so we passed the time pushing our children on the swings in my backyard. She had an open invitation to play on our swing set anytime whether I was home or not. One day toward the end of a long week, I completely lost patience with my boys as we tried to get ready for soccer practice. I know I yelled at them, threw a soccer cleat and probably slammed a door. It wasn't pretty. As I hurried the boys into the car, I looked in the backyard and saw my neighbor on the play set. I was so embarrassed. My behavior did not reflect the Jesus I had tried so hard to introduce her to. I avoided her for a few days until she rang my doorbell. My husband told her I was busy studying and couldn't come to the door. "Studying, I didn't know she was in school," she responded. He explained I was preparing for a Bible study I had been asked to teach for the first time and had asked for total privacy so I could concentrate. She asked for the location, dates, and times and promised to come. I was horrified. She was near the front of the audience the next week when I taught a lesson from Matthew 5:12-14, "You are the salt of the earth. But if the salt loses its saltiness, how can it be made salty again? It is no longer good for anything, except to be thrown out and trampled by men. You are the light of the world. A city on a hill cannot be hidden. ……" Verse 16 continues, "In the same way, let your light shine before men, that they may see our good deeds and praise your Father in heaven." I felt almost physically ill as I looked at my friend in the audience. I felt like a total failure as salt and light in her world. As soon as I finished speaking she rushed into my arms. Through tears she said, "If you are good enough for God, I must be good enough for Him too." I wasn't sure how to respond to her comment until I realized what I had shown her with my invitations and activities was a performance, she saw right through it. I was trying to earn the grace of God which set an impossible standard in her mind. She needed to see Jesus accepting a tired mom having a bad day to understand that if He accepted me, flaws and all, He would accept her too. God seeks us fully aware of our offenses. He isn't surprised by them at all, but sometimes we are. In doing the *work* of God I had lost sight of the *wonder* of God. He wanted a relationship with my friend more than I wanted it for her. Instead of drawing her to Him, I was scaring her away from Him as she watched me go around in circles wearing myself out. What God did was bring me to an exit so I could slow down enough to see into her heart. Only then could I understand that she needed to see Jesus at work in my life making a difference everyday not me working for Him, trying to earn the impossible – the free gift of His grace.

When I fill my life with so much work for God I lose sight of the God of the work — I become a performer. I think the chief priests looked good, sounded good, did good but were exhausted. I know this feeling well and it's not what God wants for us. Good works, yes, but works that come out of a deep love for Christ and the motivation that rises out of devotion to Him. When we come to Christ, we are all given gifts and talents to use in the kingdom of God, but I sometimes act like I possess them all and should be all things to all people. When I fill my life with works that wear me out, my own religious history creeps into my life and I act as if I can *earn* God's favor. If I could earn it, I could un-earn it which would make my faith a sham. Ephesians 2:7-10 says "Now, God has us where he wants us, with all the time in this world and the next to shower grace and kindness upon us in Christ Jesus. Saving is all his idea, and all his work. All we do is trust him enough to let him do it. It's God's gift from start to finish! We don't play a major role. If we did, we'd probably go around bragging that we'd done the whole thing! No, we neither make nor save ourselves. God does both the making and saving. He creates each of us by Christ Jesus to join him in the work he does, the good work he has gotten ready for us to do, work we had better be doing," (The Message).

When I look in the Bible for words to describe the kind of behavior God desires in His relationship with me I hear words like seek, rest, know, be still, and experience. I have never once found a command to be frantic and feverish and full of my own plans. God does have good works that He wants me to do, but not at the expense of knowing Him. The more I know of Him the more I will know of myself; how I am wired and equipped and how He wants to use me. When my relationship with Him, strengthened in prayer and through the study of His words to me in the Bible, is my priority, my works become a place where I capture His vision, not just catch a passing glance as I rush past, performing.

Pointers

I'm afraid I have made the chief priests and teachers out to be bad guys. I don't believe they were bad, but I do believe they were dangerous. We don't know who made up this group of men or what their relationship was with Jesus later. In this story in Matthew their behavior reflected posing and performing – both dangers that are as real today as they were at the time of Jesus' birth. I don't want to be someone who settles for knowing about Jesus, but never really knowing Him like the posers. Or someone who never knows how close is close enough and wears themselves out in trying to figure that out, the performers. The uncertainty of a life lived like that is not what Jesus calls us to. Jesus wants us to live in such a way that everything we do *points* to Him.

I began this story with my own star sightings, people who were inspired by a higher calling, who know Jesus, and long for others to know Him too. There were some positive things the chief priests and teachers did that I want to model. They were serious students of the Scriptures. They were faithful in their service to the temple. Most importantly, they obeyed by taking the Word of God given to the prophets of the Old Testament, and passed it along. God did the rest. It's the kind of life I aspire to.

We can see these things when they are lived well in the life of a Christ follower. When I live in a state of constant fear and worry, it doesn't speak very well of the truth I know that God can be trusted to care for me. When I refuse to forgive someone who has wronged me or even worse, forgive myself, it says I matter more than God and my forgiveness is far more important than His. When I am unkind to those who don't look or act like I do it presents a picture of the Jesus I claim to love as a harsh judge with a critical spirit. When I spend my time working for Jesus and have no fresh insight to share that I have gained by simply enjoying His presence, it says I must earn His favor, not learn from Him. When I rejoice in the fallen state of a friend rather than grieving their failure along with them, it says I don't see myself in the same situation, as a sinner in need of the saving grace of God. I long for a life that speaks of Him. I want to live an authentic life that says I really believe everything I say about Jesus. There will always be failures, but when we admit we've been wrong, express our sorrow in word as well as walk and seek restoration we will be a witness to a watching world. Of course, there will be worries, but by bringing them to Jesus in prayer, it says I trust God to give me a place to lean on in this life and beyond that. It shows that God knows what is best for me and will bring His best to pass in my life.

I know people who value their self-made status. They are willing to speak of God because He seems big, distant, and abstract. He's Creator, they acknowledge that, but not Savior or Sustainer or Comforter. These are things that self-made people don't think they need so they stay away from Jesus because He is too personal. In the deepest parts of their hearts, they fear it will make them seem less than, or weak, or weird. Jesus was the suffering servant, but He was also the most powerful person who ever walked this earth. No amount of knowledge we share will impress, no clever sermon will sway, no story from a stranger reaches their soul, but a life lived out in obedience with joy speaks volumes. It can show them what the meekness of Christ looks like, causing them to follow you to Him. It's all about being a pointer.

As we've seen, posers point to the law, which leaves no room for grace. Performers point to themselves, which leaves those around them trying to measure up to a false notion that God's love can be earned. Pointers simply live for Christ in every area of their lives watching Him work in the lives of others as they travel on their road trip and journey toward Jesus.

Keep Traveling
Chapter 4 – Heartless Head Men

1. What is your definition of grace?

   In Christianity it means the free and unmerited favor of God shown toward men; the condition of being favored and sanctified by God.

   Does this sound to you like something that must be earned through good deeds or hard work?

2. Do you have a list in your mind that must be checked off or you feel like you are in trouble with God? Who sets the standard and determines the value of your effort?

3. Ephesians 2:8 says, "For it is by grace you have been saved through faith – and this not for yourselves, it is the gift of God – not by works, so that no one can boast." Meditate on this verse and ask God to open your mind to the idea of His grace freely given to you. If you were to accept

His grace, think about what a difference it would make in your life — no more striving, no more anxious wondering if you've done enough, and no more trying to measure up. Write down your thoughts as you ponder this.

4. Think about the examples of those in the chapter who stopped short of going the distance to Jesus. Which struggle do you most relate to?
   • wrong conclusions
   • poor information
   • a struggle to trust
   • fear of suffering
   • religious history

5. Make a list of your religious activities. In a parallel column, make a list of the spiritual insights you have gained just by spending time with God in prayer or the study of His word. The insight list should be longer. God wants your wonder to lead to work, not your work to replace the wonder. Think about what changes you might

need to make to restore freshness to your relationship with Christ.

6. What does your life point to? What do you want it to point to? What do you need to get it there?

Chapter 5

Boys Will Be Boys
The Magi

W hen my youngest son was not quite two I was carrying him down the carpeted stairs of our home in Houston when I slipped: bare feet, big hurry, and bad idea. In my best effort not to hit his head on the wall I leaned left, landed on his leg and broke it. Or, it broke. His brothers went to swim team practice the next day practically shouting, "Guess what my mom did to my brother!" I've had better days. When we went to the doctor he took one look at all four of my boys crowded into the examining room and said, "You'd better take a few of my cards, you'll be back." My babe ended up in a blue cast with glow-in-the dark stripes — our first cast. Who knew there were options?

All summer long he walked with his leg at a very strange and painful-looking angle so he could at least touch his toes to the ground. In addition to wearing the cast, he wore the same outfit, every day – no flex. It was jean shorts, the same jean shorts, every day, no shirt, one shoe, and two capes – every day. He wore one batman and one superman cape — a boy needs to be prepared, just in case. We spent most of that summer at the baseball field watching the older boys. I am not the best sports watching mom because I get distracted by my own friends in the stands and spend more time chatting than I do watching. I was chattering away to a friend when I heard an older man at the end of the bleachers say, rather rudely, "Oh dear, look at that poor little crippled kid walking out on the field, where is his Mother?" That would be *me*. I turned around as fast as I could and frantically yelled for my son to come back. The other players weren't paying much attention, the umpire hadn't noticed him yet, and the game was carrying on when he turned around, pointed his finger at me and yelled as loudly as he could, "I just need to tell my brother sumpin." (That's something for those who don't read toddler.) Two of the older boys were playing in the outfield and he needed to tell them something. Simple as that.

Wandering

I see the Magi in that story. They were learned men of royal rank who had a childlike faith. They were men of wonder.

Children are simple, elemental, and uncomplicated. They get right to the heart of things and act on what they know, even if it's not all they need to know. My son did that when he hobbled out on to the ball field. He had a need to talk to his brother and he got right to the heart of it with no regard for risk. The Magi saw what they needed to see as they studied the night sky, and they acted on it. They took steps and began a road trip. They weren't sure where they were going but started moving, toward Jesus. This is more than Herod or the priests had done.

Like children who trust easily and obey more quickly, the Magi had to learn to trust as they left home with more questions than answers, asking directions and setting out to follow a star in search of a king. They were truly "wise men."

The Magi were like children in the way they saw the celestial happenings in the sky, understanding that they pointed to Jesus, not to Caesar. They asked frank questions, combining the answers with a sense of mystery and wonder, enabling them to see things differently

In the book of Mark, Jesus is quick to scold his disciples when they try to keep the little children from touching Him. "People were bringing little children to Jesus to have him touch them, but the disciples rebuked them. When Jesus saw this, he was indignant. He said to them, 'Let the little children come to me, and do not hinder them for the kingdom of God belongs to such as these. I tell you the truth, anyone who will not receive the kingdom of God like a little child will never enter it.' And he took the children in his arms, put his hands on them, and blessed them." Mark 10:13-16. He celebrated childlike faith and cautioned the disciples about the danger of losing it. The Magi were certainly ahead of their time.

Have you ever thought about why nativity scenes have three wise men? The truth is there could have been many, we don't know. I have a set from Africa that has some extra figures, carrying instruments. They could be additional wise men, or maybe a band, who knows. The fact is that it is assumed there were three wise men because there were three gifts.

We also don't know exactly where they started out but Scripture says, "The East," (Matthew 2:1) and "The East" is a big place. Many believe it was Persia, but others believe Asia. Both are possible, but the gifts they brought were all items found in Asia. It is likely they didn't start out together, but met up along the way as they passed through towns on their journey. This is so different from the scene I imagined as I read the story. I pictured a group of friends or co-workers at an outdoor gathering, perhaps a cookout, seeing the star and packing their bags. Calling out "road trip," like we did on Friday afternoons in college, and mounting their camels. They were actually men of uncommon intelligence — scholars and scientists who studied astrology, philosophy, and even medicine. They were probably men of some wealth and stature, not to ruin your nativity scene, but men like this usually traveled with an entourage on horseback. In an effort to be historically accurate with my nativity sets, I just moved the camels off to the side and added a horse or two from the cowboy set my children used to play with. The camels were probably used to carry supplies, so they do have a presence.

Christmas cards featuring the Magi will never look the same to me. In most of the illustrations I have seen, the wise men are colorfully dressed in regal robes, traveling together on camels, and often wearing crowns. This doesn't sound much like the wardrobe of weary travelers. What may have started out as a deeply-colored cloak loses its luster after days and weeks of riding in the dust. The other thing I notice in modern-day illustrations of the wise men is that they are really, really tall. Maybe that's how they found each other along the way. Very tall men wearing crowns and stained glass coats would be easy to spot even on the crowded streets of a city during festival season. Word about their presence would surely travel quickly.

It is possible they were from the same order of astrologers as the Old Testament prophet Daniel and were familiar with his story. We don't know what religion they practiced, but they were not Jewish. Isn't it interesting that these non-Jews were the ones who set out in obedience to find the King of the Jews?

I tend to pursue those who look, act, and believe like I do. I think God wants more from me. He wants me to find Him first and then go to those who don't know Him and show them where He is. It's not about what church, what religion, or what tradition, it's about *who* God is and *how* He makes Himself known to all.

By the time the wise men find Jesus, He is a child, not an infant. Matthew 2:2 says "We saw..." *not* we see it every day. In my imagination the star moved a little each day and they followed as it moved. I don't think it was like that. Matthew 2:2 says, "We saw his star when it rose and have come to worship him. " Perhaps the star rose and was visible when Christ was born, but wasn't seen again until after the Magi met with Herod. Jesus was a toddler by the time they arrived in Bethlehem. They were no longer in a stable, but living in a house. After Herod's plans were thwarted by the Magi's return home by another route, he had all of the two-year-old boys killed. "When Herod realized that he had been outwitted by the Magi, he was furious, and he gave orders to kill all the boys in Bethlehem and it's vicinity that were two years old and under, in accordance with the time he had learned from the Magi" (Matthew 2:16). To me this means Jesus was that age at the time of the Magi's visit. The journey from the East was long, maybe as long as two years. With only a direction to head and no specific destination in mind they couldn't have known the length of their journey when they began. When they set out, their expectations were probably very different from the reality that unfolded along the way. Isn't it amazing that the Bible is full of everyday truth? This story is ancient and yet current. It reminds me of all of times I expected my prayers to be answered quickly and they weren't.

The Magi had a star, some history, their knowledge, but not much else. They probably planned as best they could but still had to set out with great uncertainty and continuing on no matter what. In their part of the world, the weather had all kinds of extremes and challenging difficulties like sand storms. If the sky was cloudy or the sand was blowing, they wouldn't have been able to see the star even if it did travel ahead of them the entire way. If it was shining at Jesus' birth and then didn't appear again until later, they would have had to travel great distances through great difficulty without that bright encouragement. Their journey was hard sometimes, just like ours. No amount of wealth or knowledge, both of which they had, could stop a sand storm. No entourage is big enough when discouragement takes root along the way and the journey seems never-ending. Then there are the small irritants left over after the storm has passed — sand that finds its way into very uncomfortable places, much like the difficult people that are part of our daily lives. Life is filled with uncertainty and danger we cannot anticipate. We don't know how long the trip will be, who we will meet along the way, or exactly where to go next, but we do have a *star* of our own. Jesus.

Wondering

The star stayed. That is one of the characteristics mentioned in science, retrograde motion, and the Scriptures, "it stopped over the place where the child was" (Matthew 2:9). Just because I do not see Christ at work in my life or my world, doesn't mean He's not there. It means something is obstructing my view. It could be the world which preoccupies and distracts me to the point that I stop looking. This happens when I want things I don't have and probably don't need. "Things" become the center of my attention and I begin to wander off on my journey toward Jesus. This is so easy to do in our world today and confirmed by culture. More, more, more. The Magi probably wanted a hot bath and a warm meal and clean clothes and a comfortable bed many times throughout their journey, but if they let their wanting overwhelm them, they would lose their way.

When I have done something wrong and need to confess my sin, God makes it very clear to me. One way He does this is by showing me my thought life. It happens when I am easily disappointed and discouraged. When I try to figure out why, I realize I am spending my mental energy, which saps my physical energy, staring at the very thing I'm trying not to look at. I find myself comparing and coveting instead of finding the contentment that God desires for me. When I look around at everybody else, it appears that the women in my life are wearing deeply-colored stained glass robes like the Magi are wearing in the Christmas cards and while I'm wearing a cloak covered with dust. I covet a life that seems easier than mine and begin to want the life God has given to someone else. The comparison game is the worst kind of trap for women. Glass breaks; no life is shatter free. There are broken pieces just underneath the surface for everyone, but so often I'm looking at everything else but Jesus, and I dismiss the hardships of others, forgetting to be grateful for the many, many blessings that are mine.

If I've hurt someone's feelings, I avoid them. Fear fills my heart as I watch the caller ID. If they seek me out, I may be forced to face my failing. If I've overspent the budget and my husband wants to talk about it, I manipulate both the situation and the conversation trying to cover up my failure. If I've lied, I lie some more to hide the truth. The possibilities are endless. Until I confess my sin, both in prayer to God and to the person I've wronged, my view of Christ will not be clear. The Bible speaks of this in 1 John 1:9, "If we confess our sins, he is faithful and just and will forgive us our sins and purify us from all unrighteousness."

He hasn't hidden Himself from me; I've hidden myself from Him. The Magi would not be able to see the star if they never looked up at the sky.

There must have been cloudy days on the journey to Bethlehem when the Magi may have felt like they lost the star. It's a bit scary when the only thing you are following seems to be out of sight. This happens to me when I run ahead of God. I think I know my way and live like it, but I don't. I make decisions and then ask God to bless them instead of waiting, studying what Scripture says, praying, and talking to those godly people whose advice I trust. The reason the star seems in a shadow is because I've cast my own over it and run ahead.

There were probably times along the way when the star was not visible. For reasons known to God alone, this not only happened then, but it still happens to us today. We have prayed faithfully. We have studied hard. We have talked to every godly person we know. We have confessed, totally —but still no star comes into view. I have learned from experience and see it again through this study of the Magi that the best thing to do at times like these is to keep going in the same direction you were already going. Just put one foot in front of the other and persevere. Until you have a new direction, just keep going in the direction God has already given to you. I believe it was the stops along the way that helped the Magi at moments like these. Imagine starting out on a journey by yourself and then suddenly running into someone who has the same information you do and is going in the same direction when you stop over for supplies.

Or you come into a new town asking questions only to find yourself in the company of someone who has experienced just what you have. There is so much comfort in support even if it's found in a really tall stranger wearing a crown! We are not meant to journey alone, especially on the journey toward Jesus. Help is everywhere. You just have to be looking!

When I don't see God at work in my life, when circumstances are hard and my prayers seem to go nowhere, I look to others who are doing well. Their path is easy, for now, and they are enthused by the clear direction of God in their lives. My pastor-husband is fond of telling people, "If you don't have any hope of your own, borrow mine." I believe God puts us in community, among friends and in families, for this very reason, so we can borrow each other's hope. When I cannot see God at work in my own life — which happens sometimes — I am encouraged to see Him at work in the lives of those around me until my hope is restored and I can see the star again – which always happens.

When the Magi arrived in Jerusalem they moved among the crowd asking, "Where is the one who has been born king of the Jews? We saw his star in the East and have come to worship him" (Matthew 2:2). This is the reason their journey ended well. They *never* stopped looking at Jesus and were not afraid for the watching world to know it. Their hardship brought glory to Christ, which is exactly how it should be. Suffering with a purpose makes suffering purposeful.

When the Magi arrived in Jerusalem and saw the festival atmosphere they probably thought the crowd was celebrating the birth of Christ just as they were. Wrong. News of any king other than Herod was alarming to the people because they knew Herod's history and what he was capable of. "When King Herod heard this he was disturbed, and all Jerusalem with him" (Matthew 2:3). Despite the distress, the Magi carried on. They met secretly with Herod; got the information they were looking for and went on their way.

Worshipping

According to the Scripture, "when they saw the star, they were overjoyed" (Matthew 2:10). I know what overjoyed looks like in a young boy; it's a fist pump and a chest bump. It's their arms thrust in the air and their mouth open wide because of the excitement of what's just happened – the score was made, the trick was landed, the test was passed, the girl said yes—it's more than the body can contain, it simply overflows.

I don't know what overjoyed looks like when you are a scholar from the East, but based on the words of Matthew 2, it looks like a bow, at least on the outside. I'll bet there was some dancing on the inside, after all boys will be boys, but on the outside there was humility, there was an acknowledgement that this young child before them was the King of Kings and Lord of Lords. The world would never be the same because God in heaven had chosen to send this child to earth to save His lost people. No words of exchange are recorded because I imagine the Magi are both speechless and slack-jawed. Everything God showed them in the sky had led them here. The success of their journey speaks to the character of God and the integrity of His words. God *can* be trusted. He is who He says He is and will do what He says He will do, even when we can't see it happening.

In my nativity set one wise man is standing, one is bending over in the process of kneeling, and the other one is completely kneeling. All have their heads bowed, but only the third one is on his knees. Out of all of them, I like him the best. He reminds me of what this is all about. The first one, who is standing up, keeps falling over which is actually the right posture for someone to have when they come face-to-face with Jesus. He seems to fall over by accident, which is how we feel too when we find it too hard to stand up in our circumstances. His position is not an accident. God uses every aspect of our lives, our successes, our sins, our choices, and their consequences to help us fall over flat on our faces before Him. When pride, our past, and our possessions keep us from looking up, He helps us to find our way down. We will have no choice but to begin our own personal road trip, our journey toward Jesus. We have nothing to offer but ourselves and that is all He wants. That's what He's been waiting for. I love that the wise men bowed and worshipped Jesus and *then* they offered Him their treasures. It's easy to think the treasure must come first and that we need just the right gift or we won't be accepted. We can spend all our effort and energy trying to manufacture a life that will be acceptable to God only to discover that this kind of life is exhausting. As women, too often we spend our energy trying to figure out if we've done enough when Christ says "enough" the moment we do what the Magi did, *bow.* It's the posture of surrender that says, "I am not worthy to be in Your presence, but I am. Because You invited me when You placed a star into my life to show me the way to You, and then stayed until I found the way there. I am enough because You were enough Jesus and You chose to make the ultimate sacrifice — Your death on the cross — for me." Accepting this makes us acceptable, instead of offering treasure, we become treasure.

The Magi did bring gifts – each with a special significance as they pointed to who Jesus was.

The gold, a precious and valuable metal, would have been an appropriate gift for a king because it represents royalty. It is also the most flexible of all metals. I found this intriguing. One ounce of gold can be hammered, very carefully, into a 300-square-foot sheet of golden foil without breaking into pieces. It's a metal that bends, like Jesus. He is a king, yes, the very King of Kings, but He's also a king of a different kind. He bends, not His will to ours, but down to us. He left His place in heaven to come to earth to be what we could not, a perfect sinless sacrifice for His perfectly sinful people. "But God demonstrates his own love for us in this: While we were still sinners, Christ died for us" (Romans 5:8). Gold also represents divinity. Jesus was God, in the flesh – divinity wrapped in humanity. He never became less God to become man, but He did choose to bend, to humble Himself for us.

Philippians 2:6-11, The Message, says it like this:

Think of yourselves the way Christ Jesus thought of himself. He had equal status with God but didn't think so much of himself that he had to cling to the advantages of status no matter what. Not at all. When the time came, he set aside the privileges of deity and took on the status of a slave, became human! Having become human, he stayed human. It was an incredibly humbling process. He didn't claim special privileges. Instead, he lived a selfless, obedient life and then died a selfless obedient death — and the worst kind of death at that: a crucifixion.

Because of that obedience, God lifted him high and honored him far beyond anyone or anything, ever, so that all created beings in heaven and on earth — even those long ago dead and buried — will bow in worship before this Jesus Christ, and call out in praise that he is the Master of all, to the glorious honor of God the Father.

Gold is precious and of great worth, the perfect gift for Jesus, a king worth worshipping. The second gift was Frankincense. Frankincense is a type of incense burned in the temple, the most holy place in the lives of the Jewish people. It represents God's holiness. I can't see holiness as a tangible object, but I can see what it does in someone's life — it changes everything. We use scented candles these days to change the fragrance of a room, incense works the same way. When I think of incense, I think of the smoke and the smell both of which are hard to contain. They are pervasive in their presence as they spread throughout everything. When we bow in worship before Jesus, we take Him in. The expression "inviting Jesus into your heart" comes to mind here. It's a phrase used to describe entering into a relationship with Christ. You simply humble yourself, accepting your own powerlessness, acknowledging your need for God's power and inviting His presence to take charge of your life. It's no longer me, but *Him!* When given free access, His holiness cannot be contained. It overflows from Sunday morning to every morning, from your head to your heart, and into your world.

Holiness asks the question, "Would Jesus be here, do this, think this, or say that?" It brings light into the darkest places of our hearts and, much like the smoke and smell of incense, changes the fragrance of a room. Holiness changes every aspect of our lives.

The Final gift was Myrrh. Myrrh is a spice used in the embalming process. It also represents bitterness, suffering, and affliction. The Magi were looking at the face of a child, a small boy. Yet somehow they knew that even as the King of Kings He would lead a life of great sorrow, paying the price with His very life. I think of Mary in the book of Luke as she and Joseph bring the baby Jesus to the temple to consecrate Him as was the custom. They meet an old man named Simeon who had spent his lifetime following stars he could not see — waiting for Jesus. He blesses the family and after he describes the life Jesus is destined to live, he says to Mary, "And a sword will pierce your own soul too" (Luke 2:35).

The third gift, Myrrh, is often mixed with wine and used as an analgesic to ease suffering. It was offered to Christ on the cross, but He did not take it. This breaks my heart. He knew the suffering He would endure on our behalf — the rejection and the affliction — yet He chose not only to come for us, but to fully participate. He didn't want His suffering eased so that He could experience the depth of it, and fully ease ours.

We have a Savior who has experienced every aspect of our lives. He knows our pain, our joy, our hurts, and our hardships which makes Him the ultimate traveling companion. "For we do not have a high priest who is unable to sympathize with our weaknesses, but we have one who has been tempted in every way, just as we are—yet was without sin" (Hebrews 5:15). He's walked the path, obeyed the detours, overcome the enemy, and knows the way home – but we must make the choice to follow Him. The alternative is an eternity without Him and all that He is, the source of all that is light all that is good, all that is peaceful and all that brings joy.

At the beginning of the story, it appears the Magi didn't start out together, but they ended up that way. Matthew 2:12 says, "And having been warned in a dream not to go back to Herod, they returned to their country by another route." That's possessive and singular. They had seen a common star which sent them along different routes through different life experiences to a common Savior. Nothing would ever be the same. A life touched by Jesus will change, because when all of God takes up residence in all of us, how can we not be different? Not just for eternity, but for now. We will have the same heritage, the same family, and the same past. We may have the same path set out before us with the same circumstances. The road I have traveled so far is the raw material from which God chose to make me, *me*. The difference is that having met Jesus, having entered into a relationship with Him and taken His name, I will look upon all that is past, present, and future and *see* Him. A journey with Jesus doesn't just assure my future in heaven, it affects my life every day and in every way. There will still be sin, control issues, and the desire to earn my way to heaven. I may even still struggle with doubts, but they bring me to my knees where God wants me. It's the same place the Magi found themselves, on their knees before Him recognizing who He was and who they were not. For all of us, when we begin to look at things differently, we will see something different.

God showed me something different as I looked deeply into Matthew 2 preparing my heart for Christmas. He showed me the peace-less life of Herod as he stayed stuck on a roller coaster ride by his desperate need for control. He showed me the futility of the chief priests and teachers of the law as they rode in the endless circles of a round-a-bout never quite sure where to exit and settling for close without going the distance. And He showed me the Magi, men of wisdom combined with wonder that followed the light to the feet of their Savior, and bowed in surrender.

Their road trip didn't end at the house in Bethlehem; it was just the beginning of a journey that lasts for this lifetime, and the next. He tells us in John 14:6, "I am the way and the truth and the life. No one comes to the Father except through me." Jesus is the way off the roller coaster. Jesus is the truth about the roundabout. Jesus is the light that leads to life.

Keep Traveling
Chapter 5 – Boys will be Boys

1. What surprised you most as you learned more about the Magi?

2. What does child-like faith look like to you? Does the thought of faith appearing childish bother you?

3. What keeps you from seeing Christ at work in your life?

- I'm not looking for Him, I am fine.
- I'm too busy looking at things.
- I can't see past my own sin; I feel unworthy of Him.
- It doesn't feel like He is working.

The first step toward change is recognizing you need to change. Do you? If you want to see Christ at work in your life think about what changes you could make based on the examples in the Magi chapter.

4. The Magi found companionship on the darkest part of their journey by talking to others about the star they could no longer see and finding the courage to continue as a result.

Think about your own behavior when you are struggling with faith. Are you more likely to talk to someone you can trust or isolate yourself? What can you learn from the example set by the Magi?

5. Will you bow in as the Magi did and recognize your need for a Savior?

Here is a simple prayer of surrender you can pray:

<u>Hello</u> God, I recognize you.

<u>I'm sorry</u> for my sins.

<u>Thank you</u> for dying in my place to settle my debt.

<u>Please</u> take over my life and make me new.

"Therefore, if anyone is in Christ, he is a new creation; the old has gone, the new has come!"

2 Corinthians 5:17

Chapter 6

Lessons from a Road Trip

"And having been warned in a dream not to go
back to Herod, they returned to their
country by another route."
Matthew 2:12

The Magi must have been in prayer about Herod
and how to respond to him. The dream was their
answer. *Go home by another route.* Sooner or later, we
all have to go home. Once we choose to follow "the
star" – Jesus Christ – home, He will make us into a new
woman in the midst of our old life. 2 Corinthians 5:17
says, "Therefore, if anyone is in Christ, he is a new creation; the old has gone, the new has come!" Becoming
new in Christ is one thing, daily living in the newness

of that life with Christ is another. In this chapter, we'll look at the lessons we've learned along the way that will help us when we fall back into our old ways and find ourselves back on a roller coaster or stuck in a roundabout.

Stopping the Roller Coaster

Remember the control issues we can struggle with that lead to life on the roller coaster? When control issues begin to creep back into my life, I recognize it immediately because I become irritable, irrational, and easily angry. Even "disturbed," like Herod in chapter 2. My story could read, "Elizabeth was disturbed and all of the Murphy men with her." I won't be able to stop the ride until I can *think* clearly. It's always in the mind where I need to begin. As I replace my thoughts with the thoughts of Jesus, the very words of Scripture, the transformation happens. And if I let Him change my thinking, I "see things differently." To do this, I memorize Scripture having verses that I can recall easily and others I have to look up – they are all incredibly powerful. Psalm 139: 17 says, "How precious to me are your thoughts, O God! How vast is the sum of them!" By literally emptying my mind of the controlling thoughts that preoccupy it and filling the space left behind with God's Word, I become more like Christ.

One passage that continues to be extremely helpful is Ephesians 6:13-18. It lays out the armor of God that is available to us as Christians – it's the equipment we need if we're going to get off the roller-coaster of the mind. The first piece of the armor is the helmet of salvation, which keeps us from losing our minds. In The Message paraphrase of the Bible it says, "Be prepared. You're up against far more than you can handle on your own. Take all the help you can get, every weapon God has issued, so that when it's all over but the shouting you'll still be on your feet. Truth, righteousness, peace, faith, and salvation are more than words. Learn how to apply them. You'll need them throughout your life. God's Word is an indispensable weapon. In the same way, prayer is essential in this ongoing warfare. Pray hard and long. Pray for your brothers and sisters. Keep your eyes open. Keep each others' spirits up so that no one falls behind or drops out." Once we can think clearly, the release continues as we continue in prayer. For all relationships to grow there has to be good communication. It's the same in our relationship with Christ. He hears every word we say and even the words we don't. He is attuned to our hearts. In prayer we become attuned to His. Surrender is so much easier when there is trust which comes out of the intimate conversation of prayer. Then, we must worship. I am reminded of the Magi on their knees before Jesus. Kneeling is one posture of worship It says 'thy will be done, not mine." That is the essence of surrender and the release of control. It's where we begin if we're to get off the roller-coaster and travel toward Jesus.

Exiting the Roundabout

Exhaustion is not flattering in a follower of Jesus. He gives us gifts to use for His glory but He doesn't give all of them to one person. When I find myself worn out from going around in circles it's usually because I pretend He did, *to me*. Somewhere along the way, I have slipped back into my past which tells me I must *earn* the grace of God and that the praise of men is more important than the praise of God. At this point, the best way for me to exit the roundabout is to begin *in my mind* as I mentioned above. I need to empty my mind of my own words and fill it with the words of Scripture. Ephesians 2:8 reminds us, "For it is by grace you have been saved, through faith — and this not from yourselves, it is the gift of God — not by works, so that no one can boast." You can repeat this over and over again, sometimes out loud. Then ask God to remind you what your gifts are. If we're using them well, for the glory of God and not the praise of men, we will be energized rather than exhausted. That's always a good test.

I use the list exercise from the end of chapter four (page 108) and make a list of my activities and a parallel list of insights. If I have no insights to offer because all my energy is used up in activities, I know I'm in trouble. When you're lost, it's always best to find your back by going back to the beginning, to the basics. I like to call them landmarks.

Landmarks

I have no sense of direction at all so I navigate by using landmarks. My sister lives in the country surrounded by roads with poor signage and names instead of numbers. I am constantly lost as I try to go to and from her house. I know I'm lost, but not sure how I got that way or how to get back to where I started so I look for landmarks. I *can* remember the name of the bank on the corner, which side of the road it's supposed to be on and that I am supposed to pass it early in my journey. When I'm lost, I think about the bank. Which side of the road *was* it on? How long ago did I pass it? These questions help get me back on track. Landmarks work in the journey toward Jesus too. Here are some key ones:

Quiet/Devotion Time

An important landmark throughout your journey toward Jesus will be a time of quiet devoted to your relationship with God. These days my house happens to be the quietest early in the morning but that hasn't always been the case. There have been times when waking up before my family was impossible so I would use the afternoon when my boys were sleeping for my "quiet time." However, I wasn't always that flexible. I have often felt that unless my day *began* with this time I was doing something wrong. I let that bother me to the point where I felt if I missed the morning I had let God down. It's true that God wants my undivided attention so I can hear Him well enough to talk to Him in prayer and deepen my relationship with Him by reading His Word, but He doesn't mind if I set a time that is best for me. I think He prefers it. There are times when there is no quiet at all. In this case, find the quietest place and time and then quiet your heart. Ask God to help you tune out the distractions and listen to Him. He will. This time is vital because it's so personal. All of the great sermons, worshipful Christian music, and well-written Christian books cannot take the place of this time devoted to your relationship with God. In the chapters of this book, I have spoken of taking your concerns and questions to God in prayer – this is the time to do that. This time needs to be personal for you and your own individual lifestyle. For example, I always begin with coffee mostly because it's warm and hard to drink when I am moving. It's the first step toward getting me to sit still. I start out reading from a devotional book (there are endless choices) and read in my Bible the Scriptures that go along with the day's devotion. This prompts me to pray. Sometimes I pray on my knees or sometimes just sitting in a chair. (I pray really well while I walk my dog, too!) There are no magic words. There is no pre-determined amount of time required to make your time "official." Just pray. I often write prayers in a journal so that I can keep track of what I've prayed for. It somehow helps me release control of my concerns when I take them out of my mind and onto a page. This is the type of old journal I refer back to when the stars don't seem to be shining in my life anymore. I have several journals that I have used in dark times where I have gone back and added dates and details next to items on my list of prayer requests. It reminds me over and over again of how faithful God has been in the past and how creative He is in dealing with my worries. It gives me much-needed confidence to keep going and a reminder to keep looking up.

Prayer

I find prayer very difficult to describe. It's a bit like describing the love I have for my husband. Words are inadequate because it's deeply personal. It's the kind of relationship that is so special it must be experienced in order to be explained. Prayer is like that. When developing your prayer life, it's best to just begin. I find it works well when I start with the proper perspective. You can begin your prayers with talking to God about who He is. Scripture is full of descriptions of who God is — powerful, present, faithful, omniscient (He knows everything), omnipresent (He sees everything), compassionate, forgiving, just, merciful, etc.. Then take time to thank Him for what He's done. This is different from focusing on who He is. His character is unchanging. He will still be powerful even if He chooses not to use that power the way you want Him to. Then spend time in confession, saying you're sorry. When I struggle, I say, "I'm sorry, I'm not sorry," and wait for the Holy Spirit to stir my heart. Confession is for us, not for God. He knows all and doesn't need to be shown our sin, He wants us to see it and acknowledge it, so He can forgive, not condemn. The price has been paid, there are consequences, but there is no condemnation.

Then I present my requests to Him. John 14:1 says, "Do not let your heart be troubled. Trust in God; trust also in me." Let this be your guide for requests. If something troubles your heart in any way, I consider it a request. Nothing is too small or too large. Whatever troubles your heart may not be the same as what troubles mine, but that doesn't matter. God is interested in every area of your life.

Many times my prayers are as organized like what I've described above, but many times they are frantic and fearful. Sometimes I can't think in sentences, so I pray in words like *please and help*. When it's really bad I pray in gasps and tears. God sees this, hears me, and honors my prayers no matter how I have delivered them to Him. He has promised in Psalm 34:15, "The eyes of the Lord are on the righteous and his ears are attentive to their cry:…". Remember Jesus did not take the Myrrh mixed with wine at the cross so that He could fully experience our suffering. He still does, as we bring everything to Him in prayer.

Bible Study

Bible study is another important landmark we need in our lives. I get the most out of the Bible when I study it systematically, starting at the beginning of a book and studying it in small sections until the end. I have spoken at many retreats and conferences where I am asked to facilitate a chat time. During a session like this, one woman told me that she reads her Bible every day by holding it in her hand, saying a prayer, letting it fall open in her lap, and reading from whatever page is open before her. The next day she does the same thing rarely landing in the same place twice. Her question to me was, "is this okay?" The Word of God is so powerful that even the smallest amount of time spent in the most obscure part can have an impact. God can do His most with our least. But I think what this woman was really asking me, "Is there more to this?" As I silently prayed for words that would help her, God gave me the mental picture of a driveway made out of stone. It reminded me of this woman's Bible study method. Every day she laid one stone next to another until over time she built a driveway. It gave her a place to stand

and kept her on her feet, but it wasn't very helpful for the hard places in life. A set of stairs would be much more useful. If we read the Bible in a systematic way, starting at the beginning of a book and reading to the end, a little at a time, we build a structure placing stone upon stone. This provides not only strength, but also depth and a solid set of stairs we can use to climb over the obstacles in our path. When I stand at the end of my driveway I cannot see around the corner or past the trees on either side. It is a solid place to stand, but my view is limited. When I get a ladder or step stool and look at things from a higher plain, my perspective changes entirely. I can see my husband's car coming around the corner. I can see my boys and their friends coming on their bikes. I can also see storm clouds on the horizon. Some of the things I see are exciting, others are frightening, but I can see. When we open and shut our Bible according to our will it is as if we are telling God what we will let Him teach us, but if we allow Him to build daily on what we learned the day before a bigger picture begins to unfold.

My teacher friend from chapter 2 taught me to ask questions when I study the Bible. I read the verses and then ask:

1 – Is there a command to obey?

2 – Is there a warning to heed?

3 – Is there a promise to obey?

4 – What have I learned about God from what I've studied today?

5 – What have I learned about myself?

This method gives structure to my study time. The other aspect of Bible study that I try to practice is meditating on God's word.

Meditating on God's Word

There are many ways to meditate on the Word of God. It's a discipline that allows the Scriptures to "take hold" in our hearts and minds. Here are a few suggestions:

- Take time to read a verse or passage in the Bible over and over.
- Begin to memorize all or part of the verse.
- Listen – quiet your heart to allow the Holy Spirit to speak to you through God's Word.
- Consider how it fits with the rest of the Bible and life in general.
- Move to application and connect your thoughts to action. Consider how the truth and power of the Word of God should affect your behavior.

Returning to Their Country by Another Route

The Magi didn't start out together, but they ended up that way. Don't try to travel this journey on your own Find a church that teaches the Bible and a group of fellow travelers to accompany you along the way. You'll not only go deeper with God, but you'll have so much more fun along the way.

Jesus has already come *for* you; it's time for you to come *to* Him. It begins for you as it did for the Magi, with just one step toward Jesus. It's not a long trip, travel well.

Acknowledgements

M any thanks to Woody who gave me a book that made me think, Tom who gave me a swift kick to get me started, Larry who gave me the final encouragement to jump off the cliff and to Angela, Holly and Terry – the women who love them.

To Gwen and Steve – thanks for sending me to the longing bench. This book is a result.

To Barbara and Tim – thanks for letting me start this journey at your Father's world. Kluth's on the Bay is truly a sacred place.

To Shelly – this would have been so much less without you. You edited, encouraged and entered the throne room on my behalf. Thank you.

To my prayer team – I am grateful beyond words.